THAT THE WORLD MAY KNOW™

FAITH LESSONS 6–10

Raynard Vander Laan

PUBLISHING

Colorado Springs, Colorado

THAT THE WORLD MAY KNOW ™: Leader's Guide 2, for Faith Lessons 6–10

Copyright © 1996 by Raynard Vander Laan

ISBN: 1-56179-413-9

Published by Focus on the Family, Colorado Springs, CO 80995.
Distributed in the U.S.A. and Canada by Word Books, Dallas, Texas.

Focus on the Family books are available at special quantity discounts when purchased in bulk by corporations, organizations, churches, or groups. Special imprints, messages, and excerpts can be produced to meet your needs. For more information, write: Special Sales Department, Focus on the Family Publishing, 8605 Explorer Drive, Colorado Springs, CO 80920; or call (719) 531-3400 and ask for the Special Sales Department.

Editor: Michele A. Kendall
Text Design, Black-and-White Maps, Diagram on p. 94, and Overhead Transparency 6: B.C. Studios
Overhead Transparencies 7, 8, 9, 10, and 12 and Illustration on p. 110: Charles Shaw
Overhead Transparency 11: Ritmeyer Archaeological Design
Cover Design: Marvin Harrell
Cover Map: Weslight
Photographs on Front Cover: Jim Whitmer
Photograph of Author on Back Cover: Patrick Brock

Printed in the United States of America

96 97 98 99/10 9 8 7 6 5 4 3 2 1

CONTENTS

Overhead Transparency Masters: 1. The Middle Eastern World
  2. Topography of Israel
  3. The Valley of Jezreel
  4. Israel
  5. The Divided Kingdom
  6. Chronology of Bible Times
  7. Baal Sacrifice Altar
  8. The Goddess Asherah
  9. The Siege of Lachish
  10. Destruction of the High Places
  11. The First Temple at Jerusalem
  12. The Temple at Arad

OPTIONAL FULL-COLOR OVERHEAD-TRANSPARENCY PACKET

(see inside front cover for ordering information)

1. The Middle Eastern World
2. Topography of Israel
3. The Valley of Jezreel
4. Israel
5. The Divided Kingdom
6. Chronology of Bible Times
7. Baal Sacrifice Altar
8. The Goddess Asherah
9. The Siege of Lachish
10. Destruction of the High Places
11. The First Temple at Jerusalem
12. The Temple at Arad
13. The Entrance to the Water Shaft on Tel Megiddo
14. The Water Tunnel of Megiddo
15. The Ancient Wall Blocking the Cave of the Spring at Megiddo (Outside View)
16. The Ancient Wall Blocking the Cave of the Spring at Megiddo (Inside View)
17. The Water Shaft of Hazor
18. The High Place and Altar at Dan
19. The Altar at Megiddo
20. The Valley of Jezreel Viewed across the Altar at Megiddo
21. The Temple Mount at Jerusalem
22. The Cave of the Spring of Gihon
23. Hezekiah's Water Tunnel
24. The Midway Point in Hezekiah's Tunnel Where the Workers Met
25. A Wadi in the Negev
26. Flood in the Wadi
27. Quiet Waters in the Wilderness
28. Tel Arad
29. Panorama of the Temple at Arad
30. The Outer Court of the Temple at Arad
31. The Holy Place of the Temple at Arad
32. The Holy of Holies of the Temple at Arad

Full-Color Maps: ....*Mike Ginsburg Productions*
Overhead Transparency 6: ....*B.C. Studios*
Overhead Transparencies 7, 8, 9, 10, 12: ....*Charles Shaw*
Overhead Transparency 11: ....*Ritmeyer Archaeological Design*
Overhead Transparencies 13, 16, 17, 18, 19, 22, 23, 26, 27: ......*Eyal Bartov*
Overhead Transparencies 14, 15, 20, 24, 25, 28–32: ....*Raynard Vander Laan*
Overhead Transparency 21: ....*Courtesy of Greg Holcombe*

"THAT THE WORLD MAY KNOW . . ."

More than 3,800 years ago, God spoke to His servant Abraham: "Go, walk through the length and breadth of the land, for I am giving it to you" (Genesis 13:17). From the outset, God's choice of a Hebrew nomad to begin His plan of salvation (which is still unfolding) was linked to the selection of a specific land where His redemptive work would take place. The nature of God's covenant relationship with His people demanded a place where their faith could be exercised and displayed to all nations so that the world would know of Yahweh, the true and faithful God. God showed the same care in preparing a land for His chosen people as He did in preparing a people to live in that land. For us to fully understand God's plan and purpose for His people, we must first understand the nature of the place He selected for them.

In the Old Testament, God promised to protect and provide for the Hebrews. He began by giving them Canaan—a beautiful, fertile land where God would shower His blessings upon them. To possess this land, however, the Israelites had to live obediently before God. The Hebrew Scriptures repeatedly link Israel's obedience to God to the nation's continued possession of Canaan, just as they link its disobedience to the punishment of exile (Leviticus 18:24–28). When the Israelites were exiled from the Promised Land (2 Kings 18:11), they did not experience God's blessings. Only when they possessed the land did they know the fullness of God's promises.

The land God chose for His people was on the crossroads of the world. A major trade route, the Via Maris, ran through it. God intended for the Israelites to take control of the cities along this route and thereby exert influence on the nations around them. The Promised Land was the arena within which God's people would serve Him faithfully as the world watched. Through their righteous living, the Hebrews would reveal the one true God, Yahweh, to the world. (They failed to accomplish this mission, however, because of their unfaithfulness.)

Western Christianity tends to spiritualize the concept of the Promised Land as it is presented in the Bible. Instead of seeing it as a crossroads from which to influence the world, modern Christians view it as a distant, heavenly city, a glorious "Canaan" toward which we are traveling as we ignore the world around us. We are focused on the destination, not the journey. We have unconsciously separated our walk with God from our responsibility toward the world in which He has placed us. In one sense, our earthly experience is simply preparation for an eternity in the "promised land." Preoccupation with this idea, however, distorts the mission God has set for us. That mission is the same one He gave to the Israelites. We are to live obediently *within* the world so that through us, *it may know that our God is the one true God.*

Living by faith is not a vague, other-worldly experience; rather, it is being faithful to God right now, in the place and time He has put us. This truth is emphasized by God's choice of Canaan, a crossroads of the ancient world, as the Promised Land for the Israelites. God wants His people in the game, not on the bench.

The geography of Canaan shaped the culture of the people living there. Their settlements began near sources of water and food. Climate and raw materials shaped their choice of occupation, dress, weapons, diet, and even artistic expression. As their cities grew, they interacted politically. Trade developed, and trade routes were established.

Biblical writers assumed that their readers were familiar with ancient Near Eastern geography. Today, unfortunately, many Christians do not have even a basic geographical knowledge of the region. This series is designed to help solve that problem. We will be studying the people and events of the Bible in their geographical and historical contexts. Once your students know the who, what, and where of a Bible story, they will be able to better understand the why. In deepening their understanding of God's Word, they will be able to strengthen their relationships with Him.

Terminology

The language of the Bible is bound by culture and time. Therefore, understanding the Scriptures involves more than knowing what the words mean. We need to understand those words from the perspective of the people who used them. The people God chose as His instruments—the people to whom He revealed Himself—were Hebrews living in the ancient Near East. These people described their world and themselves in concrete terms. Their language was one of pictures, metaphors, and examples rather than ideas, definitions, and abstractions. Where we might describe God as omniscient or omnipresent (knowing everything and present everywhere), a Hebrew preferred: "The Lord is my Shepherd." Thus, the Bible is filled with concrete images from Hebrew culture: God is our Father and we are His children. God is the Potter and we are the clay. Jesus is the Lamb killed on Passover. Heaven is an oasis in the desert, and hell is the city sewage dump. The Last Judgment will be in the Eastern Gate of the heavenly Jerusalem and includes sheep and goats.

Several terms are used to identify the land God promised to Abraham. The Old Testament refers to it as Canaan or Israel. The New Testament calls it Judea. After the Second Jewish Revolt (A.D. 132–135), it was known as Palestine. Each of these names resulted from historical events taking place in the land at the time they were coined.

Canaan is one of the earliest designations of the Promised Land. The word probably meant "purple red," referring to the dye produced from the shells of murex shellfish along the coast of Phoenicia. In the ancient world, this famous dye was used to color garments worn by royalty. The word for the color eventually was used to refer to the people who produced the dye and purple cloth for trade. Hence, in the Bible, *Canaanite* refers to a "trader" or "merchant" (Zechariah 14:21), as well as to a person from the "land of purple," or Canaan. Originally, the word applied only to the coast of Phoenicia; later, however, it applied to the whole region of Canaan. Theologically, Canaanites were the antithesis of God's people, and therefore the opposition between the Israelite and Canaanite was total.

The Old Testament designation for the Promised Land derives from the patriarch Jacob, whom God renamed Israel (Genesis 32:28). His descendants were known as the children of Israel. After the Israelites conquered Canaan in the time of Joshua, the name of the people became the designation for the land itself (in the same way it had with the Canaanites). When the nation split following the death of Solomon, the name *Israel* was applied to the northern kingdom and its territory, while the southern land was called Judah. After the fall of the northern kingdom to the Assyrians in 722 B.C., the entire land was again called Israel.

The word *Palestine* comes from the people of the coastal plain, the Philistines. Though *Palestine* was used by the Egyptians long before the Roman period to refer to the land where the Philistines lived— Philistia—it was the Roman emperor Hadrian who popularized the term as part of his campaign to eliminate Jewish influence in the area.

Today the names *Israel* and *Palestine* are often used to designate the land God gave to Abraham. Both terms are politically charged. *Palestine* is used by the Arabs living in the central part of the country, while *Israel* is used by the Jews to indicate the State of Israel. In this study, *Israel* is used in the biblical sense. This choice does not indicate a political statement regarding the current struggle in the Middle East, but instead is chosen to best reflect the biblical designation for the land.

Introduction to the Study

Because God speaks to us through the Scriptures, studying them is a rewarding experience. The inspired human authors of the Bible, as well as those to whom the words were originally given, were Jews living in the ancient Near East. God's words and actions spoke to them with such power, clarity, and purpose that they wrote them down and carefully preserved them as an authoritative body of literature.

God's use of human servants in revealing Himself resulted in writings that clearly bear the stamp of time and place. The message of the Scriptures is, of course, eternal and unchanging—but the circumstances and conditions of the people of the Bible are unique to their times. Consequently, we most clearly understand God's truth when we know the cultural context within which He spoke and acted and the perception of the people with whom He communicated. This does not mean that God's revelation is unclear if we don't know the cultural context. Rather, by learning how to think and approach life as Abraham, Moses, Ruth, Esther, and Paul did, modern Christians will deepen their appreciation of God's Word. To fully apply the message of the Bible to our lives, we must enter the world of the Hebrews and familiarize ourselves with their culture.

That is the purpose of this curriculum. The events and characters of the Bible will be presented in their original settings. Although the videos offer the latest archaeological research, this series is not intended to be a definitive cultural and geographical study of the lands of the Bible. No original scientific discoveries are revealed here. The purpose of this series is to help students better understand God's revealed mission for their lives by allowing them to hear and see His words in their original context.

This curriculum provides additional cultural background and biblical material for study. Encourage your students to read the appropriate Bible passages and to think through God's challenge for their lives today.

Guidelines for Leading the Sessions

1. Be sure to read through the curriculum and view all the videos before you begin teaching the sessions. To lead this study effectively, you will need to spend several hours preparing for the course. In addition, you will need time to set up your class materials and to decide which activities you will use in each session, depending on the time you have allotted for the course.

2. Develop the answer you want your students to reach for each question, but during class allow them to arrive at their own conclusions before you present yours. This is the essence of the "guided discussion" method. The most effective way to discover the Bible in its setting is for the teacher to be a fellow learner with the class. Cultivate discussion and guide students in their conclusions by becoming adept at asking the kinds of questions that will help them explore different answers. Most important, encourage your students to respect the responses of others.

3. At the beginning of each session, review the key materials. Students need time to absorb and integrate the new information into their understanding of the Scriptures. If you occasionally review important locations on maps, refer to people and events in the biblical chronology, and repeat the main points in previous lessons, students will develop the ability to read the Bible in context. It is also important for you as the teacher to be well versed in the basic cultural background of the Bible. Consider memorizing key details on the maps and in the chronology.

4. To learn more on the cultural and geographical background of the Bible, consult the following resources:

   History
   Bierling, Neal. *Giving Goliath His Due: New Archaeological Light on the Philistines.* Grand Rapids: Baker Book House, 1992.

   Wood, Leon. Revised by David O'Brien. *A Survey of Israel's History.* Grand Rapids: Zondervan, 1986.

   Jewish Roots of Christianity
   Wilson, Marvin R. *Our Father Abraham: Jewish Roots of the Christian Faith.* Grand Rapids: Eerdmans, 1986.

   Geography
   Beitzel, Barry J. *The Moody Atlas of Bible Lands.* Chicago: Moody Press, 1985.

   Gardner, Joseph L. *Reader's Digest Atlas of the Bible.* New York: Reader's Digest, 1993.

General Background

Alexander, David, and Pat Alexander, eds. *Eerdmans' Handbook to the Bible.* Grand Rapids: Eerdmans, 1983.

Butler, Trent C., ed. *Holman Bible Dictionary.* Nashville: Holman Bible Publishers, 1991.

Archaeological Background

Mazar, Amihai. *Archaeology of the Land of the Bible: 10,000–586 B.C.E.* New York: Doubleday, 1990.

5. To learn more about the specific backgrounds of the second set of videos, consult the following resources:

Ackerman, Susan. "Sacred Sex, Sacrifice, and Death." *Bible Review* (Feb. 1990): 38.

Bivin, David. "'Jehovah'—A Christian Misunderstanding." *Jerusalem Perspective* (Nov./Dec. 1991).

Bleibtrau, Erika. "Grisly Assyrian Record of Torture and Death." *Biblical Archaeology Review* (Jan./Feb. 1991): 52.

Borowski, Oded. "The Carmel: Formidable Barrier and Wedge in the Sea." *Bible Review* (Oct. 1990): 46.

———. "The Negev—The Southern Stage for Biblical History." *Bible Review* (June 1989): 40.

Briner, Bob. *Roaring Lambs: A Gentle Plan to Radically Change Your World.* Grand Rapids: Zondervan, 1993.

Choon-Leong, Seow. "The Ineffable Name of Israel's God." *Bible Review* (Dec. 1991).

Cole, Dan. "How Water Tunnels Worked." *Biblical Archaeology Review* (Mar./Apr. 1980): 8.

Currid, John. "Abortion: Child Sacrifice in the '90s?" *Ministry* (Summer 1993): 2.

Dobson, James C. Monthly Newsletter. July 1993. Published by Focus on the Family.

Gill, Dan. "How They Met." *Biblical Archaeology Review* (July/Aug. 1994): 20.

Hareuveni, Nogah. *Desert and Shepherd in Our Biblical Heritage.* Neot Kedumim, Israel: Neot Kedumim Ltd., 1991.

Herr, Larry G. "An Off-Duty Archaeologist Looks at Psalm 23." *Bible Review* (Apr. 1992): 44.

Herzog, Zeev, Miriam Aharoni, and Anson F. Rainey. "Arad: An Ancient Israelite Fortress with a Temple to Yahweh." *Biblical Archaeology Review* (Mar./Apr. 1987): 16.

Hurowitz, Victor. "Inside Solomon's Temple." *Bible Review* (Apr. 1994): 24.

Kleven, Terence. "Up the Waterspout." *Biblical Archaeology Review* (July/Aug. 1994): 34.

Levy, David M. *The Tabernacle.* Bellmawr, N.J.: Friends of Israel Gospel Ministry, 1993.

Shanks, Hershel. "Destruction of Judean Fortress Portrayed in Dramatic Eighth-Century B.C. Pictures." *Biblical Archaeology Review* (Mar./Apr. 1984): 48.

Shiloh, Yigal. "Jerusalem's Water Supply During Siege: The Rediscovery of Warren's Shaft." *Biblical Archaeology Review* (July/Aug. 1982): 24.

Stager, Lawrence E., and Samuel R. Wolff. "Child Sacrifice at Carthage—Religious Rite or Population Control?" *Biblical Archaeology Review* (Jan./Feb. 1984): 31.

Usshishkin, David. "Defensive Judean Counter-Ramp Found at Lachish in 1983 Season." *Biblical Archaeology Review* (Mar./Apr. 1984): 66.

———. "Lachish: Key to the Israelite Conquest of Canaan?" *Biblical Archaeology Review* (Jan./Feb. 1987): 18.

Van't Veer, M. B. *My God Is Jahweh.* Gloucester, Va.: Paideia Press, 1980.

Wright, Rodney. "'Lachish and Azekah Were the Only Fortified Cities of Judah That Remained' (Jeremiah 34:7)." *Biblical Archaeology Review* (Nov./Dec. 1982): 72.

Youngblood, Ronald. "Counting the Ten Commandments." *Bible Review* (Dec. 1994): 30.

6. This curriculum is designed to offer you, the teacher, maximum flexibility in scheduling and pacing the sessions. Depending on how much material you choose to use, each lesson can cover anywhere from one 60-minute session to a series of four, five, or even six 60- or 75-minute sessions. For your convenience, each lesson has been divided into segments of 60 minutes each. The end of each of these segments is indicated by a row of asterisks. If you need to cover an entire lesson in just one 60-minute session, a plan for how to do that is provided under the heading "How to Plan for This Lesson" at the beginning of each lesson. In preparing your class sessions, be sure to look over the optional **Digging Deeper** sections, as you may find information there that you'll want to present, either as a supplement to the core material or—if time is limited—even in place of some core material.

NOTE TO THE TEACHER: *Some discussion sections and topics in Set 2 are repeated from Set 1. Although they are relatively few, they do provide important information for the lessons of Set 2. If you have already covered them in the first unit, a simple review is probably sufficient. If you have not completed Set 1, the sections and topics repeated here are essential background to understanding the material in this unit.*

INNOCENT BLOOD

For the Teacher

Western culture is engaged in a war of values. Secular humanists and Christians are battling for dominance, and the outcome is still in question. Determined to promote God's principles in an increasingly pagan world, Christians are becoming involved in any way they can to stop Western culture's spiritual and moral decline. One area of particular concern is society's trivialization of human life, whether of the unborn, the old, the homeless, or the terminally ill.

This conflict of values may appear to be a modern problem, but the ancient Israelites confronted similar issues when they settled in the Promised Land. Their neighbors, the Canaanites, were worshipers of Baal, and they honored him with rituals that included sacred prostitution and child sacrifice. Their lack of respect for human dignity and life clashed with the Israelites' values and beliefs, just as Christians today battle with secular society's influences. In this lesson, we will focus on Tel Megiddo, a prominent pagan high place dating from centuries before the time the Israelites entered Canaan. We will consider how the Canaanites' ungodly attitudes and practices shaped their society and how they affected the Israelites. We will also learn how God responds to oppressors of the innocent.

The main point of this lesson is to challenge your students to influence the culture around them, particularly regarding the dignity and value of human life. Ask students to think of examples of our society's lack of concern and respect for the individual and for life itself. After a few responses, help them to understand how important it is for them to be positive, godly influences on those around them.

Your Objectives for This Lesson

At the completion of this section, you will want your students:

To Know/Understand

1. The geography of the Valley of Jezreel and its relationship to the Via Maris trade route.

2. The importance of the city of Megiddo in the ancient Near Eastern world.

3. The reason Megiddo is called Armageddon.

4. The nature of the pagan religions practiced by Israel's neighbors and their effect on God's people.

5. God's anger against a society that is guilty of shedding innocent blood and perverting human sexuality.

6. The similarity between modern Western culture and that of the Israelites at the time of Ahab.

To Do

1. Recognize that a battle rages between good and evil in this world and commit to standing for God in the struggle.

2. Identify the "Megiddos" of today and commit to making an impact in these vital areas.

3. Commit to God to be more aware of the innocents of the world, whether the old, the young, the poor, the sick, the homeless, or the unborn, and to be more outspoken on their behalf.

How to Plan for This Lesson

Because of the volume of material in this lesson, you may need to divide it into several class sessions. To help you determine how to do that, the lesson has been broken into segments that can each be covered in approximately one hour. The end of each of these segments is marked by a row of asterisks.

If, however, you need to cover the entire lesson in one 60-minute session, you should include the following elements in your lesson plan:

• Step One—sections 2 (exclude questions), 3, and 4

• Step Two—sections 4, 5, and 6(c)

How to Prepare for This Lesson

Materials Needed

Student copies of the maps:	"The Middle Eastern World"
	"Topography of Israel"
	"Israel"
	"The Valley of Jezreel"
Overhead transparencies:	"The Middle Eastern World"
	"Topography of Israel"
	"Israel"
	"The Valley of Jezreel"
	"Chronology of Bible Times"
	"Baal Sacrifice Altar"
	"The Goddess Asherah"
Student copies of the handouts:	"How to Tell a *Tel*"
	"The Fertility Cults of Canaan"

Video: **Innocent Blood**

Overhead projector, screen, VCR

1. Make copies of the "Middle Eastern World," "Topography of Israel," "Israel," and "Valley of Jezreel" maps for your students.

2. Prepare the overhead transparencies "The Middle Eastern World," "Topography of Israel," "Israel," "The Valley of Jezreel," "Chronology of Bible Times," "Baal Sacrifice Altar," and "The Goddess Asherah."

3. Make copies of the handouts "How to Tell a *Tel*" and "The Fertility Cults of Canaan" for your students. (If possible, the students should receive and read these handouts before the lesson.)

4. Determine which optional **Digging Deeper** sections, if any, you want to use in your class session(s). NOTE: You can use these sections in any order you wish (e.g., you might want to use **Digging Deeper III**, but not **Digging Deeper I** or **Digging Deeper II**).

5. Review the geography of the lands of the Bible from the "Introduction."

6. Prepare your classroom ahead of time, setting up and testing an overhead projector and screen (for the overhead transparencies) and a VCR. If you plan to hand out biblical references for

your students to look up and read aloud, prepare 3x5 cards (one reference per card) to distribute before class.

Lesson Plan

Step One: "Megiddo"

1. Introductory Comments

One of the places God chose to work in human history was the city of Megiddo in the Valley of Jezreel. The city's importance can be fully understood only in light of its location: It guarded a mountain pass through which the international trade route, sometimes called the Via Maris, passed. What happened in this area, historically and culturally, was of such critical importance to the biblical story that it became the symbol of God's plan for the future.

2. Map Study: Megiddo

HINT: *With your students, review the maps of the Middle East and Israel. Identify key locales and work toward the area this lesson is dealing with—Megiddo. This will enable students to become familiar with the settings of biblical events and to be able to identify specific locations. If possible, identify ancient locations by their modern-day names.*

Using the overhead transparency "The Middle Eastern World," point out the following areas and locations, and have your students find them on their maps.

> Mesopotamia (the eastern empires of Assyria, Persia, Babylon)
> Egypt (the western empire)
> the Tigris and Euphrates Rivers
> the Nile River
> the Mediterranean Sea
> the Arabian Desert
> Israel
> the international trade route (Via Maris)

Ask your students to respond to the following questions:

- Why was the trade route so important?
- Why did the trade route pass through Israel?
- Why did God choose Israel as the land where His plan of salvation would unfold? (Allow the students time to explore the possibilities regarding God's choice of a land. Help them to see that God selected a location that was on the crossroads of the ancient world. Because of the forbidding Arabian Desert toward the east, the only trade and military route between Mesopotamia and Egypt was the corridor of Israel. That meant God was establishing His people in a place where they could be witnesses to the world that He was God.)
- What are the implications for you? Why has God put you, His follower, where you are?

Using the overhead transparency "Topography of Israel," have your students find the following areas and locations on their maps.

the coastal plain	the Jordan River
the Judea Mountains	the Valley of Jezreel

Mount Carmel	the Bashan Mountains
the Negev	the Sea of Galilee
the Galilee Mountains	

Using the overhead transparency "Israel," have your students find the following locations on their maps.

Hazor	the international trade route (Via Maris)
Gezer	
Megiddo	

Using the overhead transparency "The Valley of Jezreel," have your students find the following locations on their maps.

Mount Carmel
Nazareth
Megiddo

a. *Map Study Lecture*

The rugged mountain ranges of Samaria, Judea, and Hebron cut through the middle of Israel from north to south, making travel difficult from east to west. In ancient times, the great international trade route, sometimes called the Via Maris, entered the Great Rift Valley from the east, near Hazor. The Via Maris followed this relatively easy track until it reached the Sea of Galilee. From there, the road turned southwest into the Valley of Jezreel. The ridge of Mount Carmel barred its path to the coastal plain. There are three "gates" through Mount Carmel, but only one provided relatively easy travel: the Iron Wadi, which was guarded by Megiddo, the most significant city in Canaan.

Once past Mount Carmel, the road continued along the coast. The main branch of the road stayed inland several miles, avoiding swampland caused by runoff from the Judea Mountains. Sand dunes along the coast kept the runoff from reaching the sea. A strategic location along the Via Maris was the city of Gezer, situated where the swamps touched the foot of the central mountains. After passing this swampy area, travelers on the trade route continued south to Egypt.

In Israel, Gezer, Hazor, and Megiddo were at places on the trade route where the road could be easily controlled. They were important cities. Gezer stood where the road passed between swampland and mountain; Hazor and Megiddo stood where the road entered mountain passes. Whoever controlled the road dominated international trade and exerted great influence upon other cultures. Unfortunately, the Israelites rarely controlled these cities because their fear of the Philistines and the Canaanites kept them in the mountains. Therefore, they never exerted the kind of influence upon the world that God had intended.

b. *Guided Discussion*

HINT: *If your class is reluctant at first to offer opinions and observations, stimulate discussion by asking individual students, "What do you think, ———?" Accept their answers without judging them. Once a student offers an answer, invite other members of the class to express their views. If a student asks you, as the teacher, a specific question, instead of answering it immediately, turn it back to the student or the class by asking, "What do you think about that?" or, "Why do you think that is important?" If you are prepared and know the goal of the lesson, you can guide the discussion toward that goal. NOTE: This section contains foundational material from Set 1, Lesson 1,* **Digging Deeper IV**, *in this curriculum series.*

1. Ask your students to find the location on the map for each of the following scriptures and explain the meaning of the verse based on the strategic significance of the location.

a. Joshua 16:10a—Gezer

b. 1 Kings 9:15–17—Hazor, Megiddo, and Gezer

2. Megiddo, guarding the narrowest pass on the trade route, exerted great control over the biblical world. Ask your students to comment on the following:

a. Institutions that shape culture could be called "Megiddos." What are the Megiddos of our culture? Think of four examples. For each, briefly explain what makes it significant.

b. Whose value system controls these modern-day Megiddos? How is that value system influencing the world at large?

c. How should the fact that culture is shaped by these Megiddos affect the attitudes and actions of the Christian community? For each example of a Megiddo given in the first question above, give suggestions of ways in which the Christian community could influence it.

d. How could the Christian community encourage young people to consider a career in the areas of greatest influence in our culture? (NOTE: I strongly recommend that your students read the book *Roaring Lambs: A Gentle Plan to Radically Change Your World*, by Bob Briner. Briner believes that the Christian community has failed to participate in those institutions and activities that have the greatest influence on culture. He cites extensive examples of our failure to participate in movies, television, literature, and the visual arts. He presents an interesting proposal to encourage young Christians to pursue careers in these fields. His specific suggestions include ways to support young people and encourage them to follow God's call into these fields, how to influence television programming, how to encourage production of good literature, how to teach discernment to young people, and how to encourage colleges to prepare people to be influential in these important fields. Since he is speaking of those areas we have called the "Megiddos" of culture, his book offers excellent practical applications of this concept. It is well written and exciting to read.)

e. How might you become involved in these areas of strategic importance in the shaping of cultural values?

3. Review the Overhead Transparency "Chronology of Bible Times"

Using the overhead transparency "Chronology of Bible Times," highlight the following dates for your students:

1000 B.C.	David, Solomon
900 B.C.	Kingdom divides
	Jeroboam, Rehoboam, Omri, Ahab, Jezebel, Elijah, Elisha, Jehoshaphat
800 B.C.	Jeroboam II (Amos, Hosea, ca. 750), Joash
700 B.C.	Hezekiah, Isaiah
	Assyria destroys Samaria (north), Sennacherib attacks Judah (south)
600 B.C.	Josiah, Jeremiah
586 B.C.	Judah falls to Babylonians, people are carried into captivity

4. View the Video *Innocent Blood* (35 minutes)

HINT: *If possible, arrange your classroom setting in a semicircle around the VCR and TV so that all students are able to see and hear the presentation comfortably. Encourage your students to take notes if they wish. Ideal lighting is bright enough for the students to take notes, yet dim enough for them to clearly see the video.*

5. Guided Discussion: Pagan Practices at Megiddo

Allow your students to reflect a few moments on the video they just viewed. Then ask them to answer the following questions:

a. Why was Megiddo such an important location?

b. What was the impact of having pagan rituals practiced at such a crucial place?

* * * * * * * * * *

OPTIONAL — Digging Deeper I: Israel on the Crossroads *(9–12 minutes)*

*(NOTE: The following section is foundational material from Set 1, Lesson 1, **Digging Deeper III**, in this curriculum series. I recommend reviewing this information with your class.)*

A. Review

Israel is important not only for *what* it is—a land dependent upon God, which teaches faith—but also for *where* it is—on the crossroads of the world through which the civilizations of that time passed because there was no other route. God put His people in a public place so that the world would know them, and through them, it would know God as well. God intended the world to know who He was based on how His people lived. Isaiah 43:12 says, "'You are my witnesses,' declares the LORD, '*that I am God*'" (emphasis added). This tells us that God's people must conduct themselves in such a way that through them *the world may know* that He is God (see 1 Kings 8:60).

B. Guided Discussion

1. Have your students (individually or as a class) summarize the story and note the motivation of the key person in the story for each of the following passages (assigned on cards before class). **HINT:** *If the class is large enough, assign the passages to small groups for discussion. Allow 3 to 5 minutes maximum for group analysis.*

   a. Joshua 4:19–24

   b. 1 Samuel 17:40–46

   c. 1 Kings 18:16–37

   d. Isaiah 37:14–20

   (For further study, the following scriptures echo the same theme: Isaiah 43:12; Exodus 7:17; Judges 2:10–11; Matthew 15:29–31; Joshua 2:11; 1 Kings 8:59–60; 2 Kings 19:19.)

2. God placed His people on the crossroads of the world, not in a back alley. Challenge your students by asking them to respond to the following questions:

   a. What are some specific applications for your Christian life today? How will you live on the crossroads of the world?

   b. What is there about your life that says to others "the Lord is God"? Relate one example of someone whose life communicated this message to you and one example of a time when your life communicated this to someone else.

6. Lecture: Tel Megiddo

Ask your students to read the handout "How to Tell a *Tel*." Then point out the following items:

- Megiddo is a *tel*, a mound composed of layers (strata) of civilization. Its size and large number of strata (more than 20, often with more than one settlement represented in each one) highlight its importance. *Tels* provide us with a record of the people who lived there—often the people of the Bible.

- The mound or hill on which Megiddo was built is called *har* in Hebrew. From *har* and the name *Megiddo*, we get our English word *Armageddon*.

- Many empires fought each other near Megiddo for control of the international trade route Via Maris. Some scholars believe more battles have been fought here than at any other place in the world.

Ask a student to read aloud Revelation 16:16. Point out to the class that the passage describes a great, final battle between good and evil. Have your students answer the following questions:

a. Why would the Jewish author of Revelation locate the most decisive battle of the ages at Megiddo in the Valley of Jezreel?

b. What does this location say about the meaning of the battle?

c. Who will win the battle?

Some Christians believe that the reference to the Battle of Armageddon is symbolic, while others believe that a literal battle for world domination will take place here. Neither view is the point of this discussion. Any Jewish person living in Israel would have immediately understood the meaning of the battle simply by the location John gave in the Book of Revelation.

OPTIONAL — Digging Deeper II: The Valley of Jezreel (Armageddon)

(8–12 minutes)

A. Map Study

Display the overhead transparency "The Valley of Jezreel," and ask your students to locate the following:

> Megiddo
> Nazareth

B. Guided Discussion: Where Did Jesus Live?

Ask students to respond to the following questions:

1. Where did Jesus grow up and live until He was approximately 30 years old?

2. How far is Jesus' hometown from Megiddo and the Valley of Armageddon?

Ask students to reflect on, and discuss their reactions to, the fact that Jesus grew up seeing the valley where the ultimate battle, symbolic or real, would take place—a battle in which He would be the Commander in Chief.

At the end of this discussion, remind your class that Jesus watches our battles in confronting evil every day and is willing to be our Defender in them.

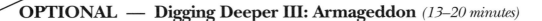

OPTIONAL — Digging Deeper III: Armageddon *(13–20 minutes)*

A. Lecture: The Final Battle

Much theological discussion centers on whether the world will end in a climactic battle between good and evil (God and the devil), in which Christians will play a significant part. It is not necessary, however, to debate whether such a battle is presently raging. It is! Some believe that the present conflict between Christian and secular value systems is Armageddon or will lead to it. Whatever your own view on the subject, focus your students' attention on the battle raging in our culture today—the battle over whose values will form its foundation.

B. Guided Discussion: What Is Our War?

Ask your students to reflect on the following questions:

1. Give a specific example of a battle over values in your community.
2. Where is our "Megiddo"? (That is, where are our battles focused?)
3. Specifically, how can you be a part of those battles?
4. What is the church's role in shaping cultural values?

C. Personal Application

Ask your students to write down one specific area where they could be more effective in the battle for biblical values. Have them discuss their answers as a class. Then spend a few minutes in prayer, asking God to give them the courage to do battle with His methods and to be encouraged by the outcome we already know.

OPTIONAL — Digging Deeper IV: King Josiah *(25–30 minutes)*

A. Lecture: Josiah's Death

One of the most stunning defeats for God's people happened in the Valley of Armageddon when King Josiah was killed in battle. Josiah was a good king, and this was a terrible loss to the Jewish people. It may be that their defeat and his death underlie the Jewish belief that good and evil will do battle here.

B. Guided Discussion: The Kings Before Josiah

Ask your students to look up the following passages to review Israel's history before Josiah's reign.

- 2 Kings 17:14–18. Because Israel (the northern 10 tribes) worshiped Baal, it was destroyed by the brutal Assyrian army during King Hoshea's reign. Only Judah remained.
- 2 Chronicles 31:1. King Hezekiah instituted reforms to prevent a similar disaster from happening to Judah.
- Isaiah 36:1 and 37:1,5–18,36–37. Because of Hezekiah's trust in God, Judah escaped (but just barely) the Assyrian army.
- 2 Chronicles 33:1–6. Hezekiah's son Manasseh returned to the Baal worship and child sacrifice that had been the downfall of Israel and nearly Judah.

- 2 Chronicles 33:21–22. Hezekiah's grandson Amon worshiped Baal as well. Things looked grim for the faithful among God's people. When would God's judgment come?

- 2 Chronicles 34:1–33. Then salvation came! Josiah, Hezekiah's great-grandson, arrived on the scene and led Israel back to faithful obedience to God. Now the power of evil would surely be defeated.

- 2 Chronicles 35:20–24. Even Josiah broke God's command when he went to fight Neco, pharaoh of Egypt. As a result, Josiah was killed by the Egyptians in the Valley of Jezreel—the plain of Megiddo. This happened in 609 B.C. Twenty-three years later, God's judgment fell on Judah in the form of the Babylonian army, which destroyed the temple and dragged the Jewish people into captivity. (See 2 Chronicles 36:15–20.)

Have the class reflect on the following:

- How could Manasseh worship Baal and allow child sacrifice when his father, Hezekiah, had sought to honor God?

- What is the implication for our passing our faith to the next generation?

- Even the godly Josiah disobeyed God's command and lost his life. What can you do to ensure that you follow God in obedience?

- God is long-suffering, but eventually His judgment does come (2 Kings 17:16–20). What significance does this have for the United States and other nations?

C. Personal Application

Ask your students if they see any "Josiahs" on the scene today. Ask them if God might be calling them to be Josiahs in their spheres of influence. After briefly discussing their answers, lead them in a short prayer, asking God to send strong leaders to defeat the power of evil.

OPTIONAL — Digging Deeper V: Tel Megiddo *(15–20 minutes)*

As was said before, *tels* are large hills that contain the remains of layers of civilization over thousands of years. They provide us with a record of the people who lived there—often the people of the Bible. (NOTE: If your students haven't done so already, they should read the handout "How to Tell a *Tel*.")

Point out the following items about Tel Megiddo:

1. The gates shown at the beginning of the video *Innocent Blood* are believed to date to the time of Solomon (tenth century B.C.).

2. The silo shown in the video is believed to be from the ninth or eighth century B.C.

3. The high place at Megiddo dates from 2950–2350 B.C., long before the Israelites arrived in Canaan. It is probably similar to the high places described in the Bible (e.g., 1 Samuel 9:12–14) and condemned so vigorously by God's prophets. (NOTE: See Overhead Transparency 19 in Lesson 7, **Digging Deeper VII**, for a view of the high place at Megiddo.)

4. The water tunnel shown in the video is believed to date from the ninth century B.C., possibly when Ahab was king. (NOTE: For a more in-depth study of Megiddo's water system, see **Digging Deeper VI** in this lesson.)

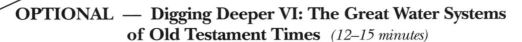

OPTIONAL — Digging Deeper VI: The Great Water Systems of Old Testament Times *(12–15 minutes)*

(This section requires the use of the optional full-color overhead-transparency packet. If you need information on ordering it, see inside front cover.)

A. Lecture

Israel is an arid country. It is hard for someone from a relatively wet climate, like much of North America, to appreciate how important water is to life in the Middle East. It is not an exaggeration to say that much of the Bible's history takes place around water. This is true in the Old Testament (note Isaac and Abimelech—Genesis 26:17–33) and in the New Testament (note Jesus' ministry near the Sea of Galilee—Matthew 4:13–14).

In the ancient Near East, cities were built only where there was a source of fresh water. When a city was small, a nearby spring, well, or cistern was sufficient. Through the years, as each settlement built upon the last and the *tel* or mound grew higher, the water source at the foot of the hill became vulnerable. To defend it from plundering armies and long sieges, the townspeople developed ways of protecting it.

In Solomon's time, a wall or corridor extended from the city wall to the spring or well nearby. But this setup was vulnerable to extended sieges. Sometime in the late ninth or early eighth century B.C., a new technology emerged: the water shaft. A huge shaft was dug through the hill and bedrock to the water table below. In some cases, a horizontal tunnel was added to the bottom of the shaft, extending outside the city wall to emerge beneath the spring. The spring (often in a cave) was then covered with large stones and soil. The water flowed unobstructed into the city, accessible in peace and war. In Jerusalem, Hezekiah's tunnel system allowed the water from a spring outside the city to flow through the mountain ridge on which the city was built and into a pool inside the city walls on the other side.

Ancient peoples spent a good part of their day obtaining water for their needs. It is difficult for us to relate to their efforts because we can get fresh water simply by turning on the faucets in our sinks. The importance of water to the people of this region underlies Jesus' promise to provide living water (John 4:13–15). When He offered the Samaritan woman water so that she would "never thirst" (verses 13–14), it was one of the greatest gifts she could ever have received.

B. Visual Insights

The following overhead transparencies give examples of some of the great water systems of Old Testament times.

Overhead Transparency 13. The Entrance to the Water Shaft on Tel Megiddo. The water source for Megiddo was a spring at the base of the hill on which this strategic city was built. From its early history through the time of Solomon, the people reached the water by walking through a small postern gate and into a gallery (a roofed hallway) that went down the side of the *tel* to the cave where the spring was located. The remains of this long, narrow extension of the city still exist where it passes through the city wall. This gallery provided security for the water supply, though during a siege the enemy could still destroy it and prevent the inhabitants from reaching it.

Scholars believe that sometime during the ninth century B.C. (Ahab is considered a likely candidate for having the vision to initiate this project), a square, vertical shaft was dug in the southwestern corner of the *tel*, through the many layers of earlier settlement and bedrock, to a depth of more than 115 feet. It was connected to a horizontal tunnel that went underneath the city to the cave where the spring was located.

This photograph shows the magnitude of the shaft and the amount of digging it took to complete the task. Steps wound around the outside of the shaft so the townspeople could reach the water. The remains of these steps can be seen just to the left of the railing, next to a modern stairway built by the Israeli Department of Antiquities. The steps were worn smooth by the feet of thousands of people who made the daily trip to draw water centuries ago. Also seen are the remains of walls originally built to keep the soil from collapsing into the shaft. The shaft seen here continues 100 feet deeper into the ground.

The great size of the shaft indicates both the strategic significance of Megiddo and the amount of effort ancient peoples expended to obtain water.

Overhead Transparency 14. The Water Tunnel of Megiddo. At the bottom of the vertical shaft, the workers of Megiddo dug a horizontal tunnel nearly 220 feet long, to the cave where the spring was located. Apparently, one crew began in the cave and another one at the bottom of the shaft. The chisel marks in the walls, still visible today, indicate that the workers came from either end to meet in the middle. How they knew the exact direction to dig, and the depth at which to begin, is unknown. But when they finished, they had accomplished one of the engineering wonders of the world. The cave was sealed from the outside, securing Megiddo's water supply from enemy attack. The city now had the convenience of a fresh water source inside its walls. Every day the women descended the shaft and walked through the horizontal tunnel to the spring. Though the tunnel shown here has electric lights and a modern walk for visitors, the people of Megiddo walked through it in near darkness. Later the tunnel was deepened so that the water flowed to the base of the vertical shaft, where water could be drawn from above.

The shaft and tunnel system of Megiddo is one of the largest and most famous of the great water systems of biblical times.

Overhead Transparencies 15 (Outside View) and 16 (Inside View). The Ancient Wall Blocking the Cave of the Spring at Megiddo. The people of Megiddo (probably at the time of Ahab) constructed this wall to hide the cave from anyone outside the city. Stairs that originally led into the cave can be seen in Overhead Transparency 16. After the wall was built, the passageway to the cave was filled with dirt so that the side of the *tel* was unbroken and there was no evidence that a cave or spring existed. The opening in the wall was made in recent times so visitors could leave the cave without returning through the tunnel.

Overhead Transparency 17. The Water Shaft of Hazor. The water system at Hazor (shown here) dates to approximately the same time as that of Megiddo but is different in one respect. The Israelites sunk a shaft nearly 100 feet through the *tel*. But instead of building a tunnel to a water source outside the city, they built a stepped passageway that led 75 feet farther down into the bedrock below the city. Here the ancient engineers found the water table and fresh water within the city's walls. The people of the city descended into the shaft on stairs around the outside (probably without railings), some of which can be seen today on the far side of the shaft, worn smooth by the feet of thousands of nameless Israelites. If the stairs were wet, drawing water probably became a dangerous task, and one wonders how many injuries or fatalities occurred as a result. The rock walls above kept the walls of the shaft from collapsing into the tunnel below.

NOTE: For information on the water system at Jerusalem, see Lesson 8, **Digging Deeper IV.**

Step Two: "Baal Worship"

1. Lecture: The Fertility Cults

Have your students read the handout "The Fertility Cults of Canaan." Emphasize the following details as background to discussion:

- Canaanite religious practices are not easily categorized, and there is debate about their exact nature.

- At heart, these pagan practices were fertility rites.

- Male and female deities were represented. The exact relationship between the deities is not clear. For our study, we will use the biblical titles of "Baal" for the male deity and "Asherah" or "Ashtoreth" for the female deity.

2. Guided Discussion: Mixing Righteousness with Evil

Israel's experience with the fertility gods of the Canaanite culture began early. Ask your students to read Numbers 25:1–13 and then respond to the following questions:

a. What happened in the story?

b. What were the specific practices used in worshiping Baal of Peor?

c. What was the relationship of these practices to the worship of Yahweh, Israel's God?

d. What was God's reaction to the Israelites' pagan worship?

e. How was God's anger appeased?

Outline for your students the formula that would set the pattern for the Israelites' subsequent worship of Baal: (1) they combined the worship of Yahweh with that of Baal; (2) they incorporated immorality as part of their religious rituals; (3) they brought God's anger and judgment upon them, to the point that He threatened to destroy Israel completely; and (4) they were called back to faithfulness by God's messengers.

NOTE: The tendency to mix the true practice of following God with the pagan practices of the Canaanite culture was a continuing problem for the people of Israel. Elijah confronted this problem as part of his ministry (see 1 Kings 18:20–21; also, Lesson 8 addresses the confrontation between Yahweh/Elijah and Baal/Ahab and Jezebel).

Ask your students to list examples of people attempting to live the Christian life but continuing in sinful attitudes or practices (in the church and in private life). Discuss some examples with the group.

OPTIONAL — Digging Deeper VII: Israel and Baal *(10–12 minutes)*

It is hard to imagine how entrenched Baal worship became among God's people during Israel's history. Put students in small groups and have each group look up a set of the following passages. Ask the groups to briefly summarize each passage and draft a short conclusion about the impact of pagan practices on Israel's culture and on God's dealings with His people.

Throughout the period of the Judges, Israel persisted in worshiping Baal.

1. The Judges: Judges 2:10–15, 3:7, 6:24–27, 10:6–7

Even Solomon turned to Baal worship.

2. The United Kingdom: 1 Kings 11:1–11

Even though warned, Israel continued to worship Baal.

3. The Northern Kingdom: 1 Kings 16:29–33; 2 Kings 17:7–20

4. The Southern Kingdom: 2 Chronicles 28:1–4, 33:1–6, 36:11–14

5. The Prophets: Jeremiah 7:30–34, 19:3–9, 2:20–25; Hosea 11:1–4

Ask a student to read aloud Jeremiah 7:3–7. Stress the action God would take if Israel's worship of the Canaanite gods did not stop.

3. Guided Discussion: Israel's Descent into Paganism

Pagans worshiped Baal to ensure abundant harvests and to prevent destructive storms and droughts. At first, they offered their animals and crops as sacrifices. Eventually, that wasn't enough, and they began offering their children. Whenever a culture wanders from its roots in God's values, descent into degrading practices soon follows.

Ask your students to read the passages below and state specifically what was involved in Baal worship. Note how the Israelites gradually descended into indescribable horror.

a. Leviticus 18:24–27 and 20:1–5, and Deuteronomy 18:10. God warned His people many times to avoid the detestable religious practices of the Canaanites, particularly offering their children as sacrifices.

b. Judges 6:25–28, Exodus 32:2–8, and 1 Kings 18:22–24. Baal altars were often associated with the figure of a calf or bull, so calf worship was a first step toward worshiping Baal (note 1 Kings 12:25–33 and 2 Kings 17:16–17).

c. 1 Kings 16:31–32 and 2 Kings 16:1–4. Sadly, many of Israel's kings led God's people away from His teachings and down the path to paganism. After Ahab married the Phoenician princess Jezebel, she influenced him to move Israel formally into Baal worship. The Phoenician cult was particularly evil because, unlike other Baal cults, it actively promoted child sacrifice and ritual sexual perversion in its worship practices.

d. 2 Kings 10:25 and 17:9–12. The Israelites used Asherah poles, sacred stones, and incense to worship the Canaanite gods.

e. Scholars are divided about the extent and the nature of child sacrifice practiced by Baal worshipers. From the Bible, it is clear that child sacrifice did occur, and the number of references to it probably indicates it was practiced widely, at least during certain periods of Israel's history. See, for example, the following passages.

- 2 Kings 16:3
- 2 Kings 17:16–17
- 2 Kings 21:1–7,16
- 2 Kings 23:10
- 2 Chronicles 28:3–4
- 2 Chronicles 33:1–6
- Jeremiah 7:31–33
- Jeremiah 32:30–35
- Ezekiel 16:20–22
- Ezekiel 20:26
- Ezekiel 23:36–39—*Oholah* and *Oholibah* are nicknames for Israel and Judah. Incredibly, the people sacrificed their children to Baal on the same day they worshiped Yahweh in the temple.
- Psalm 106:34–39
- Jeremiah 19:4–6
- Isaiah 57:5
- Micah 6:6–8—This indirect reference likely refers to those who came to God with their firstborn.

Ask your students to reflect on the following question: What would be a similar evil practiced in our society? (NOTE: Encourage students to develop a broader view of child sacrifice than just abortion.)

Point to Ponder: Israel's descent into paganism is similar to that of the United States in the last century. Both nations gradually moved away from God down the path toward evil. If Christians in the United States 40 years ago had been told that by the 1990s abortion would be legalized, R-rated shows would be the norm on television, the number of divorces and out-of-wedlock births would more than double, the murder rate in inner cities would reach epidemic proportions, and substance abuse would touch every community, they wouldn't have believed it. Help your students understand the seductiveness of sin and how easy it is to walk into its embrace.

4. Guided Discussion: The Baal Sacrifice Altar

Prepare Overhead Transparency 7, "Baal Sacrifice Altar." No one knows exactly what the Baal sacrifice altars looked like. One commonly held view based on early Jewish tradition is portrayed here. This altar was called a "topheth," though that name later came to refer not only to the altar where the sacrifices took place, but also to the area surrounding the altar, and later to the cemetery where victims were buried. (Such a cemetery in Carthage, whose religion had the same Phoenician origin as Jezebel's, covered more than 60,000 square feet, several levels deep.) The good king Josiah destroyed the Topheth at Jerusalem (2 Kings 23:10).

Whatever form the Baal sacrifices took, they were unbelievably brutal. One ancient source described the Baal altar as a hollow bronze statue of a man with a bull's head. A fire was built inside the statue, and when the idol's outstretched arms glowed red-hot, priests placed fully conscious babies on them. As flames from the brazier below scorched the babies' naked bodies, their screams and the stench of their burning flesh must have filled the valley.

In his article "Abortion: Child Sacrifice in the '90s?" Dr. John Currid quoted a description of child sacrifice by the Greek author Kleitarchos, who lived three centuries before Jesus:

> Out of reverence for Kronos (Baal Hamon), the Phoenicians, and especially the Carthaginians, whenever they seek to obtain some great favor, vow one of their

children, burning it as a sacrifice to the deity, if they are especially eager to gain success. There stands in their midst a bronze statue of Kronos, its hands extended over a bronze brazier, the flames of which engulf the child. When flames fall on the body, the limbs contract and the open mouth seems almost to be laughing, until the contracted body slips quietly into the brazier. [1]

Ask your students to reflect on the following questions:

a. Why would people sacrifice their children like this?

b. How is it possible that an entire community could watch this horror done in the name of their gods?

c. In what ways has our culture lost its sensitivity to violence and bloodshed? Why have we lost that sensitivity?

* * * * * * * * *

5. Guided Discussion: What God Hates

a. *Lecture*

God hates idolatry and particularly that unfaithfulness to His Word that leads to the oppression of the helpless and the shedding of innocent blood. (Make sure your students recognize that even though we in Western culture are not God's "chosen ones" as Israel was, He still desires that we, and all cultures, be faithful to His values. His anger will always burn against those who trample on the blood of the innocent.)

b. *Guided Discussion*

Ask students to read the following passages and answer the questions:

- Jeremiah 7:1–8. What conditions did God tell the Israelites to meet in order to remain in the Promised Land? List them. (Note that innocent blood is listed along with justice and oppression.)

- 2 Kings 24:1–4. Why was Judah destroyed?

If possible, place your students in small groups and ask them to answer the following questions:

1. How are the weak oppressed today? How is innocent blood shed? (Be sure to broaden the perspective beyond murder, to other kinds of oppression.)

2. What is God's attitude toward those who oppress the weak and innocent?

3. What finally causes the downfall of a culture?

4. The disregard for human beings results from ungodly values in a culture. How can we regain biblical values in our culture so the assault on the dignity of human life can be stopped?

c. *Personal Application*

Ask the students to write brief statements in which:

- they commit to being more aware of those in need around them

- they commit to a specific way in which they will be better advocates (in God's way) for the weak and innocent

- they commit to bringing God's values to those around them, as a first step toward respecting all human life

Take a few minutes to ask God to give each person in the class the spiritual resolve to stand up for those in need and to promote God's values in the world.

OPTIONAL — Digging Deeper VIII: Elijah, Hezekiah, and Josiah

(20–24 minutes)

A. Teaching

During the years that Israel turned from God and followed Baal, Yahweh raised up people to lead His children back to Himself. Ask your students to read the following passages:

- 1 Kings 17–21
- 2 Chronicles 29–32
- 2 Chronicles 34

B. Guided Discussion

After the students have read the passages, ask them the following questions:

1. Whom did God raise up?
2. What kind of relationship did this person have with God?
3. How did this person try to accomplish what God asked? Was he successful?
4. A spiritual commitment like Josiah's is the only way to combat the lack of respect for human life in a culture. Can you suggest a plan for confronting our society's disregard for human life? Discuss your answer with the class.

OPTIONAL — Digging Deeper IX: Oholah and Oholibah *(8–12 minutes)*

A. Teaching

Have a student read aloud Ezekiel 23:36–39,46–47. (NOTE: *Oholah* and *Oholibah* are nicknames for Israel and Judah.)

B. Guided Discussion

Ask your students to respond to the following questions:

1. How might someone justify sacrificing his or her children and then going to worship in God's temple?
2. Can you think of a time when you were active in your church but continued to accept a sinful pattern in your life? If you desire, relate your example to the class.
3. While not diminishing the terrible sin of shedding innocent blood, is there a difference in the attitude displayed by the people of Judah and that of Christians who tolerate sinful behavior?
4. How should we respond to God's warning?

6. Guided Discussion: The Goddess Asherah

If your students have not read the handout "The Fertility Cults of Canaan," you may choose to assign it now.

a. *Lecture: Asherah Worship*

The worship of Asherah (or Ashtoreth) was a significant part of the Canaanite fertility cults that Israel found so enticing. The worship of this goddess apparently involved various types of sexual perversion, including religious prostitution.

b. *Guided Discussion: Symbols and Practices*

Have your students (individually or in small groups) read the following passages and be ready to report to the class either the symbols used or the actual practice mentioned in the worship of Asherah. **HINT:** *The passages can be assigned on cards before class.*

- Deuteronomy 7:5–6 and 12:2–3—altars, sacred stones, Asherah poles, and idols
- Exodus 34:15–16—prostitution and sacrifices to idols
- 1 Kings 14:24—male shrine prostitutes
- 1 Kings 15:11–13—male shrine prostitutes, idols, and Asherah poles
- 1 Kings 22:46—male shrine prostitutes
- 2 Kings 21:7—Asherah pole in the temple of the Lord
- 2 Kings 23:7—the quarters of the male shrine prostitutes were in the Lord's temple. The women also did weaving for Asherah there.
- 1 Chronicles 5:25—unfaithfulness to God and prostitution to idols
- 2 Chronicles 21:11–13—high places and prostitution
- Deuteronomy 23:17–18—prostitution
- Jeremiah 3:1–10—note how physical adultery became the basis for spiritual adultery. The prophets saw Baal/Asherah worship as adultery against Yahweh, Israel's husband, in part because it involved sexual practices.
- Jeremiah 2:20—high places and prostitution
- Ezekiel 16:1–3,15–34—high places, prostitution, child sacrifice, and high places in town squares
- Ezekiel 23:1–21—this is a graphic description of Israel's unfaithfulness.
- Hosea 4:10–14—high places, prostitution, idols, and drinking
- Ezekiel 43:6–7—high places, prostitution, and idols
- Micah 1:7—idols, temple gifts, graven images, prostitution
- Isaiah 57:5—prostitution and child sacrifice

c. *Guided Discussion: Paganism and Sexuality*

Prepare Overhead Transparency 8, "The Goddess Asherah." The Asherah statue shown here is typical of many clay figurines found in archaeological digs from the time of the Israelites. The figurines are generally quite small (8–12 inches high) and portray a naked, usually pregnant woman holding out her breasts. Scholars identify the figurines as Asherah idols because of their "pillar" shape. They are thought to be replicas of the life-size wooden Asherah poles mentioned in the Bible (Deuteronomy

7:5–6). This overhead transparency indicates the "modern" character of the ancient cult. Ask your students to respond to the following questions:

1. What was the attitude toward sexuality in the fertility cults?
2. How did this attitude affect the culture of the Israelites?
3. Why does paganism so often use sexual perversion as a key component?
4. How has Satan used human sexuality to undermine the biblical values of our own culture?
5. Is there a link between the shedding of innocent blood for Baal and the sexual perversion for Asherah? Why is this so? Is this true for us?
6. How can we call our culture back to biblical values?
7. Why is the issue of family so central to the future of our culture? What is the answer to strengthening godly sexual attitudes and values?

Conclusion

Once again, remember that the main point we want to make in this lesson is to challenge students to influence the culture around them, particularly regarding the dignity and value of human life. This lesson is based on (1) the importance of Megiddo in shaping ancient culture and (2) the degrading Canaanite religious practices to which Israel so easily succumbed.

Ask your students to take five minutes to write their responses to the following:

1. List three people who have influenced our culture for the Lord. What was it about their lives and spiritual commitment that made an impact?
2. Can you think of a specific example in which your commitment to Jesus Christ influenced the world around you? If so, what was it?
3. List three things you can do to influence our culture about the value and dignity of human life.

Spend a few moments asking God to empower you to influence your world for Him.

Notes

1. John Currid, "Abortion: Child Sacrifice in the '90s?" *Ministry* (Summer 1993): 2.

HOW TO TELL A *TEL*

Israel is a land of hills and mountains. In fact, the first-time visitor to the country often is amazed at how little flat land there is. After several days, most travelers will notice that Israel is dotted with a certain kind of hill, one that is particularly important to students of the Bible. This hill is called a *tel* (Hebrew) or *tell* (Arabic). With its steep sides and flat top, the hill looks like a large coffee table, especially if it is in a valley and viewed from above.

What is a *tel*, and what gives it its distinctive shape?

A SETTLEMENT BEGINS

The environment of the Middle East is harsh and mostly unsuitable for settlement. For a location to be habitable, three conditions had to exist. First, there had to be a source of fresh water, which is limited in Israel. Rainfall is plentiful in some areas, but most of it falls only during the winter months. In ancient times, many communities relied on rainwater stored in cisterns. This supply was totally dependent upon the notoriously erratic seasonal rains. If a season went by with below-average rainfall, cisterns dried up, and the people abandoned the city. If an enemy laid siege to a city, only the cisterns inside the city walls were available, and often that water supply ran out and the city fell. For this reason, communities thrived only where there was an abundant supply of springwater. Jerusalem was built next to the spring of Gihon. Megiddo, Hazor, and Gezer had tunnels dug through the bedrock to reach fresh water. Without an abundant water supply, no settlement could grow.

The second condition necessary for a community to exist was an occupation that could generate a consistent food supply. In biblical times, many settlements prospered by farming. Olive trees flourished in Judea and Galilee. Wheat was raised in the valleys of Judea and the Valley of Jezreel. Shepherds took their flocks into the wilderness, searching for pasture and water. Other cities were successful with industry. Chorazin and Ekron had large olive oil processing facilities. Jerusalem was famous for its purple dye. A few cities survived by selling supplies to travelers on the Via Maris, the major trade route through the country.

The third prerequisite for a successful settlement was a defensible location. The political climate in the ancient Near East was volatile, so cities were built on hills ringing fertile valleys. Jerusalem began on a long, narrow hill, then spread across a valley to encompass another hill. Azekah was on a hill overlooking the Elah Valley, site of David's confrontation with Goliath. These hills enabled cities to defend themselves, even during an extended siege.

When all three conditions existed—water, occupation, and strategic location—a settlement began.

A SETTLEMENT GROWS

Eventually, the settlement grew large enough to require a wall and a gate. The king or ruler would build a palace and a temple, and the people would build houses, usually haphazardly, inside the city wall. Often, a steeply sloped rampart was built against the wall to protect the hill from erosion and to keep enemies from the foot of the wall. Over time, the ramparts were replaced or covered with others. These buried walls and ramparts gave the hill its steep, straight shape.

A SETTLEMENT IS ABANDONED

As the city prospered, it became an attractive prize. Enemies would lay siege to it, sometimes penetrating the defenses and destroying the population. Armies were often brutal in their conquests. Occasionally, they remained as an occupying force, but usually they marched off, leaving behind smoking ruins. Israel's conquest of Canaan followed this pattern.

Whether because of droughts, wars, or some other reason, once-prosperous cities were sometimes abandoned. Sand carried by the relentless Middle East wind gradually covered the streets and houses. Nomads arrived, pitched their tents, then moved on. Soon the ruins blended into the landscape.

A NEW SETTLEMENT BEGINS

Even when a city was destroyed or vacated, the three conditions for life in the location remained. The water source continued or, in the case of drought, the rain returned. The farmland or pastureland was still there, and the hill still offered an effective defense. Eventually, people came back and resettled. Lacking the heavy equipment needed to remove the debris of former inhabitants, the newcomers filled in holes, gathered the larger building stones, leveled off the top of the hill, and began to rebuild on the remains of the old settlement. Soon another prosperous community developed. Inevitably, its success attracted enemies, and the cycle of destruction resumed.

A LAYER CAKE OF CITIES

Over centuries and even millennia, as each settlement built upon the last one, the hill grew higher and higher. Someone compared this growing mound of cities to a layer cake, each layer representing a civilization long since disappeared from history. Archaeologists call these layers strata (singular: stratum). Beth Shean has 18 or more strata, Jerusalem has at least 21, and Megiddo has even more. Locked within these layers are pottery, jewelry, weapons, documents, gates, temples, palaces, and houses, all waiting for archaeologists to uncover their stories.

A GIFT FROM GOD

Our belief in the Bible is based on faith in God and not on archaeological discoveries. But archaeologists can help us better understand the message of the Bible by pulling us into ancient times, making them more relevant to us today. From artifacts unearthed at *tels*, we know how people during biblical times lived, what they ate, how they worshiped, what their customs were, and many other important details. *Tels* help bring the Bible to life.

For that reason, each *tel* provides a unique gift from God to better understand His Word.

THE FERTILITY CULTS OF CANAAN

Only recently have scholars begun to unravel the complex religious rituals of Israel's Canaanite neighbors. Much of our knowledge of the origins and character of these fertility cults remains tentative and widely debated. What we do know reveals dark, seductive practices that continued to entice the people God had chosen to be His witnesses.

THE ORIGINS OF JUDAISM

The people of Israel developed their faith in the wilderness. Abraham lived in the Negev desert, where God made His covenant of blood with him and sealed it with circumcision. Moses met God in a burning bush in the desert, where he learned the greatness of God's name and received his commission to bring the Hebrews out of Egypt. God spoke to His people on Mount Sinai and reestablished His covenant with them in the Ten Commandments. Throughout the Israelites' 40-year journey in the wilderness, their Lord accompanied them, protected them, fed them, and guided them to the Promised Land. There was no doubt that Yahweh was God of the wilderness.

YAHWEH OR BAAL?

When the Israelites entered Canaan, they found a land of farmers, not shepherds, as they had been in the wilderness. The land was fertile beyond anything the Hebrew nomads had ever seen. The Canaanites attributed this fertility to their god Baal—and that is where the Israelites' problems began. Could the God who had led them out of Egypt and through the wilderness also provide fertile farms in the Promised Land? Or would the fertility god of Canaan have to be honored? Maybe, to be safe, they should worship both— Yahweh and Baal.

An intense battle began for the minds and hearts of God's people. The Book of Judges records the ongoing struggle: the Israelites' attraction to, and worship of, the Canaanite gods; God's disciplinary response; the people's repentance; and God's merciful forgiveness—until the next time the Israelites reached for Baal instead of Yahweh.

Under the kings, this spiritual battle continued. By the time of Ahab and Jezebel, the fertility cults appeared to have the official sanction of Israel's leaders. Ahab, with his wife's encouragement, built a temple to Baal at his capital, Samaria. All the while, prophets like Elijah (which means "Yahweh is God"), Hosea, Isaiah, and Jeremiah thundered that Yahweh alone deserved the people's allegiance. It took the Assyrian destruction of Israel and the Babylonian captivity of Judah to convince the Israelites that there is only one omnipotent God.

This struggle to be totally committed to God is of vital importance to us today as well. We don't think of ourselves as idol worshipers, yet we struggle to serve only God in every part of our lives. It is easy (and seductive) to honor self, possessions, fun, relationships, fame, money, and a host of other gods.

We need to learn from Israel's experience and respond to Jesus' command for total allegiance. One way we can accomplish this is to study the gods that attracted Yahweh's people 3,000 years ago.

CANAAN'S GODS

Baal

The earliest deity recognized by the peoples of the ancient Near East was the creator-god El. His mistress, the fertility goddess Asherah, gave birth to many gods, including a powerful god named Baal ("Lord"). There appears to have been only one Baal, who was manifested in lesser baals at different places and times. Over the years, Baal became the dominant deity, and the worship of El faded.

Baal won his dominance by defeating the other deities, including the god of the sea, the god of storms (also of rain, thunder, and lightning), and the god of death. Baal's victory over death was thought to be repeated each year when he returned from the land of death (underworld), bringing rain to renew the earth's fertility. Hebrew culture viewed the sea as evil and destructive, so Baal's promise to prevent storms and control the sea, as well as his ability to produce abundant harvests, made him attractive to the Israelites. It's hard to know why Yahweh's people failed to see that He alone had power over these things. Possibly, their desert origins led them to question God's sovereignty over fertile land. Or maybe it was simply the sinful pagan practices that attracted them to Baal.

Baal is portrayed as a man with the head and horns of a bull, an image similar to that in biblical accounts. His right hand (sometimes both hands) is raised, and he holds a lightning bolt, signifying destruction and fertility. Baal has also been portrayed seated on a throne, possibly as the king or lord of the gods.

Asherah

Asherah was honored as the fertility goddess in various forms and with varying names (Judges 3:7). The Bible does not actually describe the goddess, but archaeologists have discovered figurines believed to be representations of her. She is portrayed as a nude female, sometimes pregnant, with exaggerated breasts that she holds out, apparently as symbols of the fertility she promises her followers. The Bible indicates that she was worshiped near trees and poles, called Asherah poles (Deuteronomy 7:5 and 12:2–3; 2 Kings 16:4 and 17:10; Jeremiah 3:6,13; Ezekiel 6:13).

CULTIC PRACTICES

Baal's worshipers appeased him by offering sacrifices, usually animals such as sheep or bulls (1 Kings 18:23). Some scholars believe that the Canaanites also sacrificed pigs and that God prohibited His people from eating pork in part to prevent this horrible cult from being established among them. (See Isaiah 65:1–5 for an example of Israel's participating in the pagan practices of the Canaanites.) At times of crisis, Baal's followers sacrificed their children, apparently the firstborn of the community, to gain personal prosperity. The Bible called this practice "detestable" (Deuteronomy 12:31 and 18:9–10). God specifically appointed the tribe of Levi as His special servants, in place of the firstborn of the Israelites, so they had no excuse for offering their children (Numbers 3:11–13). The Bible's repeated condemnation of child sacrifice shows God's hatred of it, especially among His people.

Asherah was worshiped in various ways, including through ritual sex. Although she was believed to be Baal's mother, she was also his mistress. Pagans practiced "sympathetic magic"—that is, they believed they could influence the gods' actions by performing the behavior they wished the gods to demonstrate. Believing the sexual union of Baal and Asherah produced fertility, their worshipers engaged in immoral sex to cause the gods to join together, ensuring good harvests. This practice became the basis for religious prostitution (1 Kings 14:23–24). The priest or a male member of the community represented Baal. The priestess or a female member of the community represented Asherah. In this way, God's incredible gift of sexuality was perverted to the most obscene public prostitution. No wonder God's anger burned against His people and their leaders.

CONCLUSION

Canaan's fertility cults and practices have a parallel in our day. Western culture, for all its pride in development and technology, shows a growing disregard for the sacredness of human life and still regularly terminates it for personal convenience. And sexuality has become the goddess of much of our society, including the arts, media, music, and advertising, as if success in life depends upon sexual prowess.

Human beings haven't changed much in 3,000 years. But, then, God hasn't changed at all. He still detests the belittling of human life, whether through abortion, oppression, ethnic cleansing, or euthanasia. He abhors how we have perverted our sexuality, our godlike ability to create.

As Christians, we are called to follow in the footsteps of Elijah, Hosea, Isaiah, and Jeremiah and lead our culture back to God. Only then will human life be respected and sexuality kept within the sanctity of marriage, as God intended.

WHO IS GOD?

For the Teacher

Most people can point to a crucial moment in their lives when they recognized the reality and presence of God with startling clarity. Upon reflection, they realized that God arranged the circumstances so that He became unavoidable.

The prophet Elijah was an important element in God's plan to confront an increasingly pagan Israel with His demand for total allegiance. Elijah's intense devotion to God became the instrument that shook an apathetic people. His loyalty and willingness to share God's message with anyone—from the king in his palace to the person on the street—makes Elijah one of the biblical heroes. To meet him was to know about God.

Ask your students if they know any modern "Elijahs"—people who reflect God passionately in everything they do. What makes these people unique? What effect do they have on others?

This study of Elijah is a modern call to action against the secular ungodliness around us. It is also a clear reminder of God's demand for total devotion and commitment. The question "Who is God?" is as relevant today as it was in biblical times, and the stakes are just as high.

Your Objectives for This Lesson

At the completion of this section, you will want your students:

To Know/Understand

1. The geography and topography of Mount Carmel and the biblical events that occurred there.

2. The role of the prophet in Israelite culture.

3. The meaning of the names *Elijah* and *Elisha*, as well as these prophets' relationships to later biblical events and to our faith.

4. The significance of Elijah's actions against Baal on Mount Carmel.

5. The meaning of "high place" in the biblical world and God's use of high places.

6. The threat posed by Ahab and Jezebel to God's people, Israel.

7. The meaning of God's name and the Israelites' attitude toward it.

To Do

1. Commit to living so that others recognize the presence of God in their lives, and so that the world may know that Yahweh is the one true God.

2. Establish a goal of improving their "altars," or daily relationships, with God.

3. Apply to their own lives the importance of being God's prophets.

4. Dedicate themselves to confronting evil rather than simply retreating from it or compromising with it.

5. Praise God for the incredible reality that He alone is Lord of heaven and earth.

How to Plan for This Lesson

Because of the volume of material in this lesson, you may need to divide it into several class sessions. To help you determine how to do that, the lesson has been broken into segments that can each be covered in approximately one hour. The end of each of these segments is marked by a row of asterisks.

If, however, you need to cover the entire lesson in one 60-minute session, you should include the following elements in your lesson plan:

- Step One—sections 1–4
- Step Two—section 4

How to Prepare for This Lesson

Materials Needed

Student copies of the maps: "Topography of Israel"
                                        "Israel"
                                        "The Valley of Jezreel"

Overhead transparencies: "Topography of Israel"
                                          "Israel"
                                          "The Valley of Jezreel"
                                          "Chronology of Bible Times"

Student copies of the handout: "My God Is Yahweh"

Video: **Who Is God?**

Overhead projector, screen, VCR

1. Make copies of the "Topography of Israel," "Israel," and "Valley of Jezreel" maps for your students.

2. Prepare the overhead transparencies "Topography of Israel," "Israel," "The Valley of Jezreel," and "Chronology of Bible Times."

3. Make copies of the handout "My God Is Yahweh" for your students. (If possible, students should receive and read this handout, and re-read the handout "The Fertility Cults of Canaan" from Lesson 6, before this lesson.)

4. Determine which optional **Digging Deeper** sections, if any, you want to use in your class session(s). NOTE: You can use these sections in any order you wish (e.g., you might want to use **Digging Deeper III**, but not **Digging Deeper I** or **Digging Deeper II**).

5. Review the geography of the lands of the Bible from the "Introduction" and Lesson 6, along with the material on Baal worship from Lesson 6.

6. Prepare your classroom ahead of time, setting up and testing an overhead projector and screen and a VCR. If you plan to hand out biblical references for students to look up and read aloud, prepare 3x5 cards (one reference per card) to distribute before class.

Lesson Plan

Step One: "Mount Carmel"

1. Introductory Comments: Yahweh versus Baal

In this lesson, we are going to study a dramatic episode that includes (1) God's demand that He alone be recognized as the Lord of our lives and (2) the importance of being a living witness of God's power and presence. The story has intrigue, danger, conflict between good and evil, and the dramatic intervention of God in human history.

As we read about Elijah's confrontation with Baal's prophets on Mount Carmel, challenge your students to understand the story in light of what God was, and is, doing in history rather than viewing it simply as an adventure tale. God was determined to complete His plan for the coming of Jesus and to have His people play a specific role in bringing about that plan. The Israelites' dalliance with Baal worship was a stumbling block, and God sent Elijah (among others) to remove the obstacle from their path.

God has also given us a role to play in His plan for the coming of His kingdom. Help your students to see themselves as modern "Elijahs" who have been called by God to confront the "baals" of our world and stand as witnesses that Yahweh is the one true God.

2. Map Study: Mount Carmel

HINT: *Begin this map study session by reviewing the geography of the overall area and working down to the area the lesson is dealing with—Mount Carmel.*

Using the overhead transparencies "Topography of Israel," "Israel," and "The Valley of Jezreel," help your students find these regions and locations on their maps.

    a. "Topography of Israel":
        the coastal plain
        the Shephelah (foothills)
        the central mountains (Hebron Mountains, Judea Mountains, Samaria Mountains)
        the Great Rift Valley (Jordan River, Dead Sea, Sea of Galilee)
        the Valley of Jezreel (Mount Carmel)
        the Galilee Mountains
        the Negev

    b. "Israel":
        the international trade route (Via Maris)
        Jerusalem
        Jericho
        Samaria
        Megiddo
        Hazor
        Gezer

    c. "The Valley of Jezreel":
        the Valley of Jezreel
        the Galilee Mountains
        Nazareth
        Mount Tabor
        Mount Moreh (also Hill of Moreh)

Mount Gilboa
Megiddo
Jezreel (city)
Mount Carmel
the international trade route (Via Maris)

3. Review the Overhead Transparency "Chronology of Bible Times"

Using the overhead transparency "Chronology of Bible Times," highlight the following dates for your students:

1000 B.C.	David, Solomon
900 B.C.	Kingdom divides
	Jeroboam, Rehoboam, Omri, Ahab, Jezebel, Elijah, Elisha, Jehoshaphat
800 B.C.	Jeroboam II (Amos, Hosea, ca. 750), Joash
700 B.C.	Hezekiah, Isaiah
	Assyria destroys Samaria (north), Sennacherib attacks Judah (south)
600 B.C.	Josiah, Jeremiah
586 B.C.	Judah falls to Babylonians, people are carried into captivity

4. View the Video *Who Is God?* (26 minutes)

5. Guided Discussion: Why Mount Carmel?

Elijah's choice of Mount Carmel as the place to confront the Baal prophets was surely not random. First, because it was an elevated area, there was already an altar there (1 Kings 18:30). Second, Mount Carmel symbolized fertile splendor. Because it is near the sea and is over 1,000 feet high, the mountain receives more than 30 inches of rain per year. The name *Carmel* means "God's vineyard," an appropriate description of its fertility. Mount Carmel is the most heavily forested area in Israel. Even today its slopes are covered with olive groves and vineyards. Since Canaanites worshiped fertility gods, this lush setting was the perfect place to hold a contest between them and Yahweh to determine who really was the one true God.

Have your students look up the following verses and summarize what they say about Mount Carmel.

a. Isaiah 35:1–2—It is a splendid place.

b. Song of Songs 7:5—It is used in the writer's love song as a tribute to his lover.

c. Isaiah 33:9—As a result of a curse, the vegetation on Mount Carmel dropped its leaves. (The Arabah is a desert.)

d. Amos 1:2—Again, because of a curse, Mount Carmel withered, an unusual occurrence.

e. Nahum 1:4—As a result of a curse, Mount Carmel withered, an unusual occurrence.

NOTE: The scene for the contest between Yahweh and Baal was set on the top of Mount Carmel. When Elijah challenged Baal's prophets here, it had not rained in Israel for more than three years. Even Mount Carmel must have been desolate. The people knew that God, or perhaps Baal, was angry.

HINT: *It's important for students to understand the significance of Israel's location in the ancient Near East as the basis for this lesson. If they completed the map study section in Lesson 6, a brief review may be sufficient. If they haven't done the exercise, they should do it now.*

Step Two: "Elijah and the Prophets of Baal"
(1 Kings 18)

1. Guided Discussion: Israel's Descent into Evil

Display the overhead transparency "Chronology of Bible Times," and review the history leading up to Elijah's contest with the Baal prophets on Mount Carmel. Point out the fact that the nation of Israel had been involved in a downward spiral for a long time.

a. 1 Kings 11:9–11—God predicted the kingdom would divide because of Solomon's sin.

b. 1 Kings 12:1–24—The nation divided into north (Israel) and south (Judah).

c. 1 Kings 12:25–33—Jeroboam, the first king of Israel, started the people of the northern kingdom down the path of unfaithfulness to God.

d. 1 Kings 16:25–26—Omri, a later king of Israel, became more involved in the fertility cults of the Canaanite culture.

e. 1 Kings 16:29–34—Ahab, Omri's son, established Baal worship as the official religion of the north (Israel). Jezebel, Ahab's wife, introduced the Baal cult of the Phoenicians, one of the most evil cults of all.

f. 1 Kings 17:1–5—Elijah was sent by God to confront the Israelites' increasing sinfulness.

The path to evil is taken in descending steps, and the first step is as critical as the last. Ask your students to answer the following questions:

1. Our increasingly secular society creates the gods of pleasure and materialism, the baals of our day. Can you give examples of some steps Western culture has taken to provide these kinds of gods?

2. How did Elijah confront evil in his culture and stand up for God's values? What can we do in our culture to make a similar stand? Can you identify a modern-day Elijah?

2. Guided Discussion: Confused Israelites

Use the following passages to help your students understand the setting for Elijah's confrontation with Baal's prophets. Ask students to look them up and summarize what they say:

- 1 Kings 16:29–33
- 1 Kings 17:1–6
- 1 Kings 18:16–19
- 1 Kings 18:20–21

Help the students understand how confused the Israelites were over who God was.

* * * * * * * * * *

OPTIONAL — Digging Deeper I: Putting God First (27–37 minutes)

A. Teaching: Jericho's Curse

Have your students read 1 Kings 16:34 and Joshua 6:26.

B. Guided Discussion: Putting God First

1. Ask your students to re-read Joshua 6:18–19,24–27 and read Leviticus 23:9–14. What was God's desire concerning the first portion of whatever blessings He gave to Israel?

2. Have a student read aloud Numbers 3:11–13. What did God's desire concerning the first-fruits include? (The firstborn child of each family.) Notice here that God took the Levites as His special servants in place of the firstborn.

3. Point out these facts to your students:

   - Jericho was the "first" of God's gifts of land to the Israelites.

   - Jericho was set apart to God in recognition of His ownership of Canaan (Joshua 6:24–27).

   - To claim the city or anything found in it as one's own was a terrible sin because it denied God's right to ownership over the rest of the land (Joshua 7).

   - 1 Kings 16:34 noted that it was during Ahab's reign that a citizen of his kingdom (from Bethel) rebuilt Jericho. This assumes Ahab's consent.

4. Ask your students the following questions: What is the writer of Kings saying about Ahab's attitude toward God? Is the rest of his life consistent with this opening action? How does a believer today demonstrate (or deny) God's lordship over the world? Give specific examples. It might be appropriate for students to relate some of their examples to the class.

C. Review: Firstfruits

To understand the concept of the firstfruits, we need to know several things. First, presenting God with the firstfruits symbolizes recognition of Him as the giver of everything. As one believer said, "It's not a matter of how much of my wealth I should give to God; it's a matter of how much of His wealth I should keep for myself."

Second, the firstfruits are given to God before the whole amount is received, whether harvest, family, or land. Therefore, it is an act of faith to trust God to provide the rest.

Third, taking the firstfruits for oneself is to deny God's ownership of them and to fail to live by faith. (Ask a student to read aloud 1 Kings 16:29–34; then ask the class the following question: If Hiel of Bethel was a citizen of Ahab's country, what does the passage tell you about Ahab?)

Finally, the ruins of Jericho were to be a testimony to future generations of God's ownership of them and their willingness to live by faith.

D. Personal Application

Ask your students to reflect on the following questions. (This can be done individually or in small groups.)

1. How can we implement the firstfruits idea in our lives today?

   a. Is there some physical symbol we could display to indicate God's ownership of us and our faith? (If you have Set 1 of this curriculum, refer students to the handout *"Mezuzah"* in Lesson 3.)

   b. What two specific actions could you take to more clearly demonstrate your allegiance and submission to God? (Praying before meals in a public place? Attending church? Gathering at the school flagpole to pray? Tithing for God's work?) Have the students discuss their ideas with their groups or the rest of the class.

   c. How are we tempted to deny God's ownership of us by breaking the firstfruits idea? (Failing to keep Sunday for God? Failing to give to God's work? Not giving God credit for our blessings?)

   d. Have we, as a Western culture, been removing the signs of God's ownership from our nation? How?

   e. Is it possible God will judge our nation as He did Ahab, because we no longer testify to His ownership of us? How might this happen?

2. Spend a few minutes in prayer. Ask God to impress on us His ownership of us and every-thing we have. Let's seek His strength to help us be clearer testimonies to Him that the world may know that He is God.

OPTIONAL — Digging Deeper II: Syncretism *(18–24 minutes)*

A. Lecture: Serving Two Masters

Jezebel, Ahab's wife, was totally devoted to Baal and Asherah. She hated Israel's God and tried to eliminate His prophets (1 Kings 18:4). In contrast, Ahab, like many Israelites, tried to serve Yahweh and Baal. He was unwilling to commit to one or the other, so he worshiped both. He and his people would honor Yahweh and then go to the high places to sacrifice to Baal, burn incense under Asherah poles, and participate in sacred prostitution.

Syncretism is the combination of different forms of belief and practice. The Israelites practiced syncretism when they tried to combine God's truth with paganism. This is as evil as, if not more so than, outright unbelief. Sinful things become acceptable when they are used in God's name (e.g., the Crusaders using violence, or modern evangelists using questionable techniques to raise funds).

B. Guided Discussion: Syncretism Today

Have your students respond to the following questions:

1. Can you identify syncretism in our culture today?

2. How do Christians attempt to combine the worship of God with secular ideas? Can you think of an example of someone doing sinful things in God's name?

C. Personal Application

It is important to distinguish between using structures and ideas from the culture to communicate God's message (like using television or CD-ROMs) and adopting cultural practices without reforming their inherent moral value. Using contemporary music styles to praise God can be effective, but that doesn't mean all popular songs are appropriate for Christians. Making use of certain corporate management styles in a religious organization may make it more efficient, but that doesn't mean the whole corporate philosophy is consistent with biblical values. When Christians participate in a culture to influence and transform it, they are vulnerable to also adopting its values. Historically, Christians have wavered between the extremes of isolation (retreating from the culture and having no influence) and accommodation (becoming like the culture). Both are dangerous and disobedient. We must be like Elijah, who participated in his society while being totally devoted to God.

Have your students give examples of situations in which they struggled to be godly influences on those around them without adopting their unchristian values. (Example: going to a party where some people acted in ungodly ways.) If they feel comfortable doing so, students may relate their answers to the group.

Pray together, asking God to give each person (1) the courage to participate in a culture that desperately needs God's message and (2) the wisdom to resist its secular values.

OPTIONAL — Digging Deeper III: Review of Baal Worship

If students do not have a background on Baal worship, consider doing one or more of the following:

1. Re-read the handout "The Fertility Cults of Canaan" in Lesson 6 of this volume.
2. Review Guided Discussions 7, 8, and 9 in Lesson 6 of this volume.
3. Review Overhead Transparencies 7 and 8, with their captions, in Lesson 6 of this volume.

OPTIONAL — Digging Deeper IV: The Role of the Prophet (21–23 minutes)

A. Lecture: Elijah

Through Moses, God promised that He would send prophets to help His people remain faithful in a pagan world. Elijah was one of the greatest of these prophets. Coming at a time when Israel was growing increasingly sinful and was willingly compromising its beliefs and values, Elijah thundered Yahweh's demand for total allegiance.

B. Guided Discussion: What Is a Prophet?

God raised up prophets to call His people back to His words and ways. Ask your students to look up these passages to better understand the prophet's role:

*   Deuteronomy 18:14—God recognized the seductive nature of pagan culture.
*   Deuteronomy 18:15—The prophet would be identified as one of the people.

- Deuteronomy 18:18–19—When the prophet spoke God's words, people had to listen to him because he spoke on God's behalf. God would hold responsible anyone who did not obey.
- Deuteronomy 18:20—The prophet was held to a high standard of truth.
- John 4:19—Jesus was recognized as a prophet.

C. Personal Application

Although the future-telling element of prophecy is important, we usually focus too much on it and not enough on the voice of God calling us to faithfulness. This is unfortunate because, as Christians, we are required to call our culture to faith in God and lead others to obedience.

Ask your students to respond to the following questions:

1. Can you give an example of a modern Christian who fills the role of a prophet who calls others to faith?
2. Can you recall a time when you called someone back to faithfulness to God? If you feel comfortable doing so, relate your experience to the class.
3. How could you be more "prophetic" in this sense?

Emphasize to your students the importance of the prophet in bringing people back to faithfulness. Help them to realize that all Christians are responsible for calling others back to God.

3. Guided Discussion: The Name *Elijah*

Have your students read the handout "My God Is Yahweh."

a. *Lecture*

One element of the story of Elijah's confrontation with Baal that Western believers might miss is the importance of Elijah's name. In itself, it is a powerful communication of God's message. Help your students understand this by reviewing these points:

1. The Israelites combined pagan and godly values. They tried to serve two masters (1 Kings 18:21), which is impossible (Matthew 6:24). In a sense, they were asking, "Who is God?"
2. The word *Elijah* is composed of two Hebrew words:
   - *El* means "god" and is a general reference to deity. (Earlier, *El* was the name of the Canaanite creator-god, but by Elijah's time it referred to any god.)
   - *Jah* is one part of the word *Jahweh* (*Yahweh*) and often represents the most holy name of God (Exodus 3:14).
3. Elijah's name answered "Who is God?" with "Yahweh is (my) God." Elijah's very identity was a testimony to God's person and presence.

b. *Personal Application*

Ask your students to respond to the following questions:

1. What was Ahab saying when he mentioned Elijah's name? How do you think he felt?
2. Elijah's very identity was a testimony to his commitment to God. Can we be Elijahs in this way? In what ways could our very identities speak to someone about the person and presence of God (e.g., wearing a religious symbol, praying quietly in a public place, encouraging someone who is

struggling, having a Bible or religious object displayed in one's home, volunteering at a soup kitchen or convalescent home)? List your examples and relate them to the group.

Ask each student to write a brief commitment to at least one way of becoming like Elijah by having the public identity of a follower of Jesus. If appropriate, discuss some examples with the class. Then spend a few moments together in prayer, asking God to make each person an Elijah.

4. Guided Discussion: Elijah on Mount Carmel

Read 1 Kings 18:16–45 together as a class. Then work through the following discussion topics:

a. Elijah's challenge to the people of Israel (verse 21). (NOTE: The word translated "waver" in verse 21 comes from the same word that is translated "danced" in verse 26.)

   1. What was the sin of the people of Israel?

   2. How does this relate to our day? What would be a corresponding sin in our lives?

b. The people's response to Elijah's challenge (verse 21b).

   1. Why do you think the people said nothing?

   2. What does that indicate about their spiritual integrity?

   3. OPTIONAL: Read Joshua 24:14–18. What was the people's response to Joshua's statement that he would serve the Lord? Why did the people give such a different response than what they gave in 1 Kings 18:21b? (NOTE: This is an often misquoted passage. Joshua does not say "choose which god you want." What he says is, "Fear the Lord." Since there is no other god but Yahweh, the only option the Israelites had was to *choose to serve Him*—"But if serving the LORD seems undesirable to you, then choose for yourselves this day whom you will serve" [Joshua 24:15]. Stress to your students that Joshua's message, Elijah's message— God's message—is this: Given that there is only one God, you can choose to serve Him or choose not to serve Him.)

c. The contest between God's prophet and Baal's prophets (verse 24).

   1. Elijah challenged the key issue of the Israelites' loyalty to Yahweh, not just their immoral practices. How might his example relate to our call to stand and confront the evil in our culture? What is the root cause of immorality?

   2. Can you give specific examples of times it is easier to avoid situations than to confront things that are wrong (like pretending not to hear someone take God's name in vain)? Relate a few examples to the class.

d. Elijah's preparation (verses 30–32). There was already an altar on Mount Carmel, but it was broken and unused. The altar was the means God used to establish and maintain a relationship with His people. There they showed their commitment to Him and were assured of His hearing and forgiveness. The altar was central to their relationship with God. (Read Genesis 8:20–21 and 22:13–14.)

   1. Why was the altar broken? (Note 1 Kings 19:14.)

   2. What was Elijah doing before he sought God's action?

   3. What represents the "altar" of your life? What is the condition of your altar?

   4. Can you think of an example of how an "altar in ruins" could (or did) prevent someone from acting on God's behalf? Relate the example to the class.

   5. Read James 5:17–18. Elijah's prayer was effective, not simply because he prayed "earnestly," but because he was righteous (James 5:16b)—that is, in right relationship with God.

e. Elijah's prayer (verses 36–37). Note Elijah's motive for his request for fire: ". . . so these people will know that you, O Lord ["Yahweh" in the original], are God" (verse 37). God's people are often distinguished by their desire to act as witnesses of the truth that our God is the one true God. We are standing stones on the crossroads of life so that the world may know God. Any other motive makes our actions self-centered and not the channels of God's blessing.

1. If time allows, ask students to read aloud the following passages:

Isaiah 43:12	1 Samuel 17:46
Exodus 7:17	Joshua 2:11
Joshua 4:23–24	Isaiah 37:18–20
1 Kings 8:59–60	2 Kings 5:15

2. Ask your students to think of one person they know who lives so others may know who God is. Discuss a few examples with the class. (NOTE: Stress to your students the importance of living so that everything they do points to God and not to themselves. This is what allows a person to be God's instrument.)

f. God's answer (verse 38). This is one of the most dramatic answers to prayer ever. No rain had fallen in Israel for three and a half years. Elijah called out to his God, and suddenly out of a clear sky, a lightning bolt struck the center of the altar. (Read Leviticus 9:24 and 1 Chronicles 21:26.)

1. Have you ever seen God act in a dramatic way? If you desire, relate your experience to the class.

g. The people's response to God (verse 39) was, "*Yahweh*—He is God! Yahweh—*He is* God! Yahweh—He is *God!*" (The English translates the Hebrew *Yahweh* as "Lord.") This phrase is similar to "Elijah," which means "Yahweh is God." The point is that Elijah, in relationship with God, became His instrument. Elijah did not take or need any credit . . . he only pointed to God so that the world may know.

1. Think of an example where someone you know had a sudden change of heart. How did his or her life change? Relate the example to the class.

NOTE: God's action is the only thing that can penetrate hearts of stone. When we face those who have hard hearts, our prayer must be for God to act so that they are changed.

h. Elijah's action (verses 40–45).

1. Elijah's confrontation with evil, using the means God allowed, was absolute and total. How do you think Elijah would have confronted the evils in our culture?

With Jesus, God's instructions for confronting evil changed. Jesus modeled a new approach: He confronted sinners lovingly, always desiring to turn them from their sins. But God's hatred of evil has not changed. As His followers, we are commissioned to attack the very "gates of Hades (hell)" (Matthew 16:18).

1. Have your students (individually or in small groups) answer the following questions and relate their responses to the class:

   a. What are the most significant "baals" (evils) we need to confront today?
   b. What is the most effective method of bringing the power of God to bear against these evils?

2. Ask each student to choose one modern-day baal that concerns him or her. Each student should then write a brief strategy using the model of Elijah: challenge, confront, repair the altar, pray, and act. If the setting is appropriate, discuss some examples briefly as a class.

Spend a few moments in prayer, asking God to make each person an instrument of His power and a living witness that He is God.

* * * * * * * * *

OPTIONAL — Digging Deeper V: Elisha *(25 minutes)*

A. Lecture: Elisha ("God Saves")

Elisha followed Elijah as God's prophet. Elisha's task was to complete God's judgment on Israel begun by Elijah (1 Kings 19:15–17). Elisha's name comes from two Hebrew words: *el* ("god") and *shua* ("saves" or "salvation"). So *Elisha* means "God saves" or "God is salvation." (NOTE: *Jesus* is the Greek form of the Hebrew *Joshua* or *Yeshua*, which means "Jahweh saves" or "Jahweh is salvation." His parents surely called Him Joshua [Yeshua], not Jesus.)

B. Guided Discussion: Preparing the Way

Divide your students into groups. Ask each group to read one of the passages below and summarize how Elisha brought God's deliverance or salvation to the people. Then ask each group to relate their results to the class.

- 2 Kings 2:19–22—purified tainted water
- 2 Kings 3:4–25—rescued the Israelites from the Moabites
- 2 Kings 4:1–7—multiplied a widow's supply of oil
- 2 Kings 4:8–37—brought a Shunammite's dead son back to life
- 2 Kings 4:38–41—purified poisoned food
- 2 Kings 4:42–44—multiplied bread
- 2 Kings 5:1–14—healed a leper
- 2 Kings 6:1–7—caused an axhead to float in water
- 2 Kings 6:8–23—blinded and then trapped the Arameans
- 2 Kings 6:24–7:20—defeated the Arameans
- 2 Kings 8:1–6—predicted a famine and saved a family

Elijah prepared the way for Elisha (the prophet of salvation) in the same way that John the Baptist, whom Jesus called Elijah (Matthew 11:14), prepared the way for Jesus (who is salvation).

OPTIONAL — Digging Deeper VI: Asking for the Double Measure

(28–30 minutes)

Guided Discussion: Elisha's Double Measure

A rabbi has noted an interesting relationship between Elijah and Elisha. Whether the writer of Kings intended this connection is uncertain, but it makes for interesting study. Ask your students to look up the following passages:

a. 2 Kings 2:9–10. What is Elisha's request? Elijah's answer?

b. Note Elijah's miracles: 1. 1 Kings 17:6—fed by ravens
2. 1 Kings 17:14–16—provision of food and oil
3. 1 Kings 17:19–23—brought a dead child back to life

    4. 1 Kings 18:38—brought fire from heaven at Mount Carmel

    5. 2 Kings 1:10—brought fire from heaven

    6. 2 Kings 1:12—brought fire from heaven a second time

    7. 2 Kings 2:7–8—divided the water

c. Note Elisha's miracles:
1. 2 Kings 2:13–14—divided the water
2. 2 Kings 2:19–22—purified tainted water
3. 2 Kings 2:23–24—cursed some youths, and suddenly bears appeared and mauled them
4. 2 Kings 3:14–27—filled the land with water and defeated the Moabites
5. 2 Kings 4:1–7—multiplied a widow's supply of oil
6. 2 Kings 4:16–17—prophesied a healing of barrenness
7. 2 Kings 4:32–37—brought a dead boy back to life
8. 2 Kings 4:38–41—purified poisoned food
9. 2 Kings 4:42–44—multiplied bread
10. 2 Kings 5:13–14—healed a leper
11. 2 Kings 5:26–27—put leprosy on his servant
12. 2 Kings 6:1–7—caused an axhead to float in water
13. 2 Kings 6:16–18—caused the eyes of his servant to see God's chariots and horses of fire, and his enemy to be blinded

Elisha was one miracle short of the "double measure" he asked for and Elijah promised. Ask your students to read 2 Kings 13:20–21 (a dead man was restored to life when his body touched Elisha's bones). A fourteenth miracle! The "double measure"! (NOTE: Be sure to point out to your students that there is probably more than one way to count the miracles and that Elisha might have performed more than those recorded in the Bible. Even so, the above comparison makes for an interesting possibility.)

Ask students if they are seeking God's Spirit or if they are preoccupying themselves with other things. Pause for prayer to ask for God's Spirit as Elisha did.

OPTIONAL — Digging Deeper VII: High Places *(45–37 minutes)*

A. Guided Discussion: Their Significance and Character

Scholars debate the significance and character of what the Bible calls high places. Several things can be stated with confidence.

1. In the culture of the ancient Near East, people honored their gods at the highest points in a given area. Perhaps they believed the gods lived in these exalted places. Or they may have thought they would be closer to the gods in the heavens.

2. God forbade the Israelites to use *pagan* high places (Numbers 33:52).

3. God revealed Himself through His people's culture. Since the people of the ancient Near East honored their gods by worshiping them at high places, God allowed His people to build altars to Him (and only Him) at high places as well. For example,

   • Genesis 22:2—Abraham went to Mount Moriah (the later location of the temple).
   • Exodus 19:20—God met Moses on Mount Sinai.

- 2 Samuel 24:18–21—David built an altar "up" on the threshing floor of Araunah.
- 2 Chronicles 3:1—Solomon built the temple on Mount Moriah.
- 1 Kings 18:20—Elijah confronted the Baal prophets on Mount Carmel.

Certainly, God does not approve of the values and attitudes of pagan cultures. But it is interesting that on occasion He asked His people to reclaim something for Him that a pagan culture used for the wrong reasons. The high places were an example of this. The Israelites were allowed to employ cultural practices and ideas if they had no pagan content and were used only in God's service. Ask your students to think of examples of contemporary cultural things used by the secular world that could be reclaimed and used in God's service (e.g., television).

B. Visual Insights

(This section requires the use of the optional full-color overhead-transparency packet. If you need information on ordering it, see inside front cover.)

The following overhead transparencies review some of the high places of the Canaanite and Israelite cultures and might help explain the struggle the Israelites had in resisting paganism and its seductive practices.

Overhead Transparency 18. The High Place and Altar at Dan. The high place at Dan, in northern Israel, dates to 920 B.C., when Israel was divided into the northern (Israel) and the southern (Judah) kingdoms. The high place measured 62 feet square and was surrounded by a wall. A staircase led up to it (note staircase on right in photograph). On top of the high place were buildings that housed the shrine or "idol" that was worshiped there.

Avraham Biran, the archaeologist who directed this excavation, found evidence of three different high places on this site, all built on the same location and each contributing some of what is seen here. The earliest remains date to King Jeroboam in the tenth century B.C. As the new king of the recently formed northern kingdom, Jeroboam needed an alternative to the temple established by David and Solomon at Jerusalem. Probably built over an existing "religious sanctuary," the high place at Dan focused on a golden calf as the object of worship (1 Kings 12:26–30). The platform at that time was 60 feet long and 20 feet wide and had an altar in front of the steps. In the photograph, an iron frame outlines an altar located in the same place as Jeroboam's; on the far side of the frame are the original steps for the altar. It is amazing to look at this place and recognize the beginning of Israel's drift into pagan practices and values.

According to the biblical story, Jeroboam attempted to combine the pagan calf worship of the Canaanite culture with the worship of Yahweh. Normally, Canaanite worshipers placed the figure of the god being worshiped on or near the calf idol. Although Jeroboam's calf at Dan did not have a "god" figure on it (1 Kings 12:28), a first step into paganism had been taken when the calf was created. So, "the sin of the house of Jeroboam . . . led to its downfall and to its destruction from the face of the earth" (1 Kings 13:34). Jeroboam had opened the door to evil, making it easier for the kings who succeeded him to leave the Lord and do evil in His eyes—they walked "in the ways of Jeroboam and in his sin, which he had caused Israel to commit" (1 Kings 15:34). (See also 1 Kings 15:26, 16:7,26,31, and 22:52; and 2 Kings 10:31, 13:2,11, 14:24, and 15:9,18,24,28.) It is important to realize that (1) idolatry was officially introduced into the kingdom of Israel at this point and (2) sin—whether committed by an individual, a culture, or a nation—always begins with a first step and ends with complete compromise of the truth.

Ask your students to respond to the following:

1. Think of an example of small "first steps" that have led (a) the church, (b) our nation or culture, and (c) you personally into greater sin. Discuss these examples with the class.

2. Why is the first step into sin so crucial?

3. Why is Jeroboam blamed for the evil done by succeeding kings who were certainly more idolatrous than he?

The archaeologist Biran discovered that the fire that destroyed the shrine of Jeroboam also turned the stones red.

At the second stage of development, the platform of the high place was rebuilt to its present size, probably by King Ahab, whose devotion to Baal is well known. Israel continued to sink deeper into pagan practices and values and further away from God.

The third stage of development came during the reign of Jeroboam II (ca. 760 B.C.). The large staircase and altar in front of the high place were added at that time. Archaeologists found only parts of the altar, including one of the horns that protruded from the four corners and part of the steps leading to it. Based on these finds, archaeologists constructed this metal frame, which shows how massive the altar was. It towered over the altars of earlier times.

During Jeroboam II's reign, Amos predicted the final destruction of the Israelite nation because of its idolatry and pagan practices (Amos 3:12–15, 5:11–15, 8:14). His message must have seemed totally out of place because Israel was at the peak of its prosperity. Thirty years later, however, the northern 10 tribes were destroyed by the brutal Assyrian army and ceased to exist as a people. Ashes and burn marks from a great fire were among the remains of this altar and high place, confirming Amos's prediction.

Overhead Transparency 19. The Altar at Megiddo. After reaching the Promised Land, the Israelites were commanded by God to destroy the Canaanite high places (Numbers 33:52) so that they would not be tempted to blend worship of the false gods of the land with the worship of Yahweh, the one true God.

This pagan altar at the high place of Megiddo was built in 2700 B.C. and was used until approximately 1900 B.C., not long before Abraham arrived in Canaan. The altar probably had been built over the remains of an earlier one. Part of the ruins of a large temple complex can be seen as well. Steps on the eastern side allowed the priest to climb onto the altar for sacrifices or other rituals. Though it is impossible to know exactly what happened here, the Bible records that Canaanite worship included the sacrifice of animals, as well as children during certain periods (Jeremiah 7:31). It also involved male and female ritual prostitution (1 Kings 14:23–24; Deuteronomy 23:17–18; Hosea 4:14). This altar represents the Canaanite practices that Yahweh's people found so seductive. Ahab and Jezebel would establish the worship of Baal in cities and towns near here (and quite possibly at Megiddo as well). The immorality of this pagan religion is paralleled in our secular culture. Ironically, this photograph was taken after a heavy rain that ancient peoples would have attributed to Baal.

Overhead Transparency 20. The Valley of Jezreel Viewed across the Altar at Megiddo. The flat, fertile Valley of Jezreel was the breadbasket of ancient Israel. It is important strategically because the international trade route Via Maris crossed the valley just below the altar and continued through the mountain pass guarded by the city of Megiddo. Because of this pass, the city and valley were probably the most important areas in Israel. In fact, the entire world could be influenced from this place because international trade was controlled here. Many bloody battles were fought in this valley as different empires tried to gain control of it.

The writer of the Book of Revelation described the battle between the forces of God and those of Satan that will characterize the end of time (Revelation 16:16). In typical Hebrew fashion, he located the battle at Armageddon, which stands for *Har Megeddon* ("the mountain of Megiddo").

The significance of this site in Hebrew history makes it clear that the battle will be for control of the world. Some Christians believe an actual battle will take place here, while others think a symbolic battle will rage (and is already raging) around the world between those who are faithful to the one true God and those who are not. Whatever you believe, the valley seen in this picture is a symbol of the final battle and of the victory that Jesus will have over Satan's legions.

As you face the evil around you, never be so focused on it (the altar and what it represents) that you do not look beyond it, to the valley (Armageddon) and what it represents (Christ's ultimate victory over Satan).

Overhead Transparency 21. The Temple Mount at Jerusalem. God despised the Canaanite high places where pagan worship was carried out. His orders to the Israelites were to destroy them (Deuteronomy 7:5; Numbers 33:52). Yet God communicated with His people through their culture. He allowed them to establish high places where *He* could meet with them. Moses met God on Mount Sinai and received the Ten Commandments (Exodus 19:17–20). Joshua went to Mount Ebal and Mount Gerizim to renew the Israelites' covenant with God (Deuteronomy 11:29 and 27:4–5; Joshua 8:30). Jesus introduced the law of His kingdom in a sermon on a mountain (Matthew 5–7).

The most significant high place in Israel used by God was the Temple Mount at Jerusalem. Jerusalem was originally built on the ridge seen across the center of this photograph. At the highest point on the ridge, where the golden dome (a Muslim mosque called the Dome of the Rock) stands, is a large platform on which the temple was built.

God instructed David to purchase this site as the location for the temple (1 Chronicles 21:14–30; 2 Chronicles 3:1–2), which Solomon later built. This temple was destroyed by the Babylonians in 586 B.C., but another one was built on the site by Zerubbabel nearly a century later (Ezra 3:3–13).

The massive walls seen in the photograph were made by Herod the Great when he began enlarging the area for the temple in 20 B.C. According to the Bible, his project was so complex, it was still being built during Jesus' time (John 2:20). It was finally completed approximately A.D. 60, only 10 years before it was destroyed again, this time by the Romans in A.D. 70.

The valley in the foreground is the Kidron Valley, which formed the eastern border of the city of Jerusalem. The city itself was to the left of the temple platform. The buildings in the distance are of the modern city of Jerusalem.

Point out to the class that we must follow God's example and communicate the gospel in terms our culture understands and by means it can relate to. But we must be careful to first remove any secular values or meanings in the process.

Ask your students to respond to the following questions:

1. What are examples of ways to communicate the gospel that would relate to the culture around us? (Examples: television, music, media, the arts)

2. When we use a cultural means (such as rock music) to communicate the gospel, how can we be sure that the secular elements of it don't corrupt God's message?

3. Think of something so inherently evil, it cannot be used. Relate your example to the class.

4. How would this concept of using the means of our culture to spread God's message relate to God's use of high places to meet His worshiping people?

OPTIONAL — Digging Deeper VIII: Elijah, Our Role Model
(14–18 minutes)

A. Lecture

Elijah seems to have been a strong follower of God. But Elijah was human, just as we are, and he needed God's blessing to be the witness he was. Sometimes it is hard for us to believe that God wants us to be like Elijah—to be Yahweh's champions against evil.

B. Guided Discussion

Ask your students to read the following passages and answer the questions. Have the students relate their experiences to the class.

- 1 Kings 18:46. After the confrontation with Baal's prophets, Elijah still had the strength to run nearly 20 miles to Jezreel. When have you felt this strong in the Lord?

- 1 Kings 19:3–4. Elijah, fearing for his life, ran into the Negev. Here he was ready to quit and die. When have you felt this alone, weak, and afraid?

- 1 Kings 19:7–8. God met Elijah's immediate need for strength—just enough for that day. When has God strengthened you so clearly?

- 1 Kings 19:10. Elijah was brutally honest about his despair, fear, and weakness. When have you been so honest with God?

- 1 Kings 19:11–13. God reveals Himself in the stillness of a whisper. When have you heard God in such stillness?

- 1 Kings 19:18. God encouraged Elijah with the presence of 7,000 other faithful believers in Israel. Have you ever felt the encouragement of the community of God in your time of despair? Did it help you?

Conclusion

The heroes of the Bible were great because they were used by God, not because they were morally or spiritually superior to us. Elijah was a human being, just as we are. He had strengths and weaknesses, good days and bad days. He needed to be corrected and encouraged by God, and he needed the support of fellow believers. His example should encourage us to become vessels of God's message and to be strong in Him. Only in that way can we be Elijahs.

MY GOD IS YAHWEH

Names are important in Western culture. Parents choose names for their children after much thought and discussion. For the rest of a person's life, he is identified by the name he was given before birth. But the significance of names in our day cannot compare with the significance of names in biblical times. Ancient peoples understood that a name expressed the essence or identity of a person. According to Proverbs 22:1, "A good name is more desirable than great riches." In the biblical world, a good name meant more than even a good reputation, because it identified the character of the person carrying it.

NAMES AND NAMING

There are three aspects to names and naming: (1) a name identifies the character of the named; (2) to name someone means the namer knows or understands the named; and (3) to name someone means the namer has authority over the named.

Identity

In the ancient Near East, a person's name identified something about the person's character or his circumstances (e.g., birth or family). Isaac's name—"he laughs"—described the response of Sarah, his mother, when God told her she would give birth even though she was elderly. Moses' name—from the Hebrew "to draw out"—was given to him after he was pulled from the Nile River. The angel told Mary to name her baby *Jesus* (actually *Yeshua*, a shortened form of *Yehoshua* or *Joshua*)—from the Hebrew "to save" or "savior"—because "he will save his people from their sins" (Matthew 1:21).

Knowledge

To name someone or something implies that the namer understands enough about the named and its circumstances to describe it and make use of it. Adam named the creatures of the earth. This meant he understood each one clearly enough to describe its character and function. (In Adam's case, he also was able to determine that none of them was an appropriate mate for him—Genesis 2:19–20.) Our word *classify* comes close to the activity of naming. So, when God tells us "I know you by name" (Exodus 33:17), it means more than that He recognizes us individually. Rather, it indicates that He understands completely who and what we are. This brings us to the final aspect of the naming process.

Authority

To name someone or something also implies that the namer has authority over the named. God changed Abram's name to *Abraham* (Genesis 17:5) because God had authority over him. Pharaoh could rename Joseph for the same reason (Genesis 41:45). This aspect of the naming process proved significant for the Hebrews when it came to their knowing and using God's name.

GOD'S NAME

To use God's name meant one understood something of His essential character and being, that one could identify and understand (know) Him. But God is the sovereign Creator of the universe. God existed before anyone or anything. Who among His creatures truly understood who He was? And who had authority over Him? Only God can understand His being enough to name Himself, and He alone has the authority to do it.

It was Moses who finally had the courage to ask God to give Himself a name. In the Book of Exodus, Moses said to God, "Suppose I go to the Israelites and say to them, 'The God of your fathers has sent me to you,' and they ask me, 'What is his name?' Then what shall I tell them?" (Exodus 3:13). God answered Moses by revealing His name to him.

Meaning

The name God gave Himself has caused much confusion and discussion. Both its meaning and its pronunciation are not entirely clear. The Hebrew letters for the name are *YHWH* (vowels were pronounced but not written in ancient Hebrew), and they appear more than 6,800 times in the Hebrew Bible alone. Most scholars believe *YHWH* is related to a root word meaning "to be present" or "to exist" and probably meant either "He creates or causes" or simply "I am (that I am)," meaning that God did not depend on anyone or anything for His existence. (Note Moses' first question to God and His response in Exodus 3:11–12: God identified Moses as the one who *depends* on God. This passage would support the idea that God's name identified His *independence* of any outside being. That makes God the ultimate source of everything that was, is, and will be.) This identification of God meant that His name could be used only of Him and for Him, because nothing else could possibly measure up to such a description.

Sacredness

The Israelites were afraid to use God's name because they might use it in ways that He had not revealed. Instead, they called Him "Lord" (Hebrew: *Adonai*), "God" (Hebrew: *Elohim*), "The Name" (Hebrew: *Ha-Shem*), or by some other title. After they returned from the Babylonian Captivity (ca. 500 B.C.), they refused to use God's name at all, out of respect and fear for what it represented—the holy God's self-description. The people simply said *Adonai* whenever the sacred name was intended.

Transliteration

By the Middle Ages, few Jewish people could read Hebrew because it was no longer their native language. The dispersion after the destruction of the second temple in A.D. 70 and the Bar-Kochba Revolt in A.D. 135 scattered the Israelites around the known world. Soon they spoke only the language of the lands of their dispersion, and Hebrew was relegated to religious matters. To help the people read Hebrew, the scribes of the period (called Masoretes) introduced a system of vowel marks to identify the sounds that had always been spoken but never written. These marks were placed below (occasionally above or between) the consonants of the text. Now even those not fluent in Hebrew could pronounce the words.

When the scribes came to the sacred name of God (*YHWH*), they did not want their readers to pronounce it because it was so holy. Instead of using the original vowel sounds (which were never written), they placed the vowel points from *Adonai* ("Lord") to indicate that the reader should say *Adonai* instead of *YHWH*. The vowels *a-o-a* were placed above and below *YHWH*. Later, the first *a* was changed to *e*, probably to prevent the reader from accidentally saying *Ya* (the first syllable of the sacred name). Unfortunately, Christian translators were unfamiliar with the Jewish people's respect for God's name. So to them, *YHWH*, with its *e-o-a* vowels, looked like *Ye* (Latin: *Ja*) *Ho WaH,* or "Jehovah," though that pronunciation was never used in Bible times. When we Christians use this name, we reveal our ignorance of our Jewish roots.

Most scholars believe God's name was pronounced "Yahweh." Modern translations use "LORD" in all capital letters to identify it. This obscures the practice the Israelites had of using part of God's name (*Yahweh*) in their children's names. Any biblical name ending with *iah* or *jah* includes part of God's name—for example, Hezekiah, Elijah, Azariah, and Isaiah. Names beginning with *Jeho* or *Jo* also use a syllable from God's name—for example, Jehu, Jonathan, Joel, and Jehoshaphat.

WHAT GOD'S NAME MEANS TO US TODAY

Certainly, God understands that modern Christians use *Jehovah* because they believe it is the name God gave Himself. Many other believers use *Yahweh* because it is closer to the Hebrew original. The main point is to recognize that only God is able to understand and describe Himself. We are dependent upon His revelation of His nature to understand Him. Therefore, we must use His name carefully. Using it to refer to things other than God—such as when we swear—is, in effect, to claim authority over God. That was Adam and Eve's sin and what caused them, and their descendants, to be exiled from the Garden of Eden.

The biblical characters whose names included reference to God, and whose very identities pointed to God, should be our role models. What they did with their names, we must do with our lives. Every aspect of our characters—our very identities—must speak of the living God so that the world may know that He alone is God.

Praise God that He revealed His name to us and granted us the privilege of using it for His glory!

THE WAGES OF SIN

For the Teacher

Surrounded by the seductive practices of Baal worship, Yahweh's people struggled to remain loyal to Him. As they tried to make sense of their circumstances and find meaning in their lives, they were repeatedly drawn toward pagan answers. The issues they dealt with weren't the critical ones, the ones they should have focused on. They worried about personal success and prosperity rather than faithfulness and obedience to God. But God was patient with them (just as He is with us today), and for generations He called them back to Himself.

In this lesson, we investigate God's perspective on Israel's struggle to remain faithful to Him and the moment when His patience finally gave out. Our focus is the ancient city of Lachish, which the Assyrian army destroyed as God's judgment upon His people. Unfortunately for the Israelites, it was too late for them to ward off God's justice. We, however, still have time.

It is important that your students identify with Israel's conflicting loyalties if they are to maximize the lessons of Lachish. Point out to them how the daily mundane concerns of this world can block the real issues they should be dealing with as Christians—their commitment to God and faithfulness to the lifestyle He approves. Help them to recognize the appeal of secular (pagan) answers to the meaning of life. If possible, bring in an advertisement that offers society's answer to making life worthwhile, such as an ad for a car or diet product. Ask your students what problem the ad presents, and what solution it poses. Then discuss what is wrong with that solution. Help the students to understand what the Israelites went through in trying to resist the temptations of paganism.

Your Objectives for This Lesson

At the completion of this section, you will want your students:

To Know/Understand

1. The geography of southern Judea in the history of Israel.

2. The history and archaeology of the city of Lachish.

3. The campaigns of the Assyrian and Babylonian armies in Israel.

4. God's choice of the faithful Hezekiah in preserving His people and Hezekiah's trust in God.

5. That because the wages of sin is a law built into God's world, God judged Israel, and this has specific implications for Western culture.

6. The meaning of the Israelites' 70 years of captivity in Babylon.

7. The geography of the divided kingdom of Israel.

To Do

1. Commit to defending their faith at the first sign of attack, rather than waiting until its very survival is at stake.

2. Resolve to become personally involved in the critical issues of their culture while God is still patient with them.

3. Formulate a plan to do everything possible in the struggle against sin and its effects and to trust God to bring the results He desires.

4. Commit to honoring God as the center of their lives and to being His instruments.

How to Plan for This Lesson

Because of the volume of material in this lesson, you may need to divide it into several class sessions. To help you determine how to do that, the lesson has been broken into segments that can each be covered in approximately one hour. The end of each of these segments is marked by a row of asterisks.

If, however, you need to cover the entire lesson in one 60-minute session, you should include the following elements in your lesson plan:

• Step One—sections 1–4

• Step Two—sections 1–3

How to Prepare for This Lesson

Materials Needed

Student copies of the maps:	"The Middle Eastern World"
	"Topography of Israel"
	"Israel"
Overhead transparencies:	"The Middle Eastern World"
	"Topography of Israel"
	"Israel"
	"Chronology of Bible Times"
	"The Siege of Lachish"
	"Destruction of the High Places"
Student copies of the handouts:	"The Palace of a Great King"
	"70 Reasons for 70 Years"

Video: **The Wages of Sin**

Overhead projector, screen, VCR

1. Make copies of the "Middle Eastern World," "Topography of Israel," and "Israel" maps for your students.

2. Prepare the overhead transparencies "The Middle Eastern World," "Topography of Israel," "Israel," "Chronology of Bible Times," "The Siege of Lachish," and "Destruction of the High Places."

3. Make copies of the handouts "The Palace of a Great King" and "70 Reasons for 70 Years" for your students. (If possible, students should receive and read these handouts before the lesson.)

4. Review the geography of Israel from the "Introduction."

5. Determine which optional **Digging Deeper** sections, if any, you want to use in your class session(s). NOTE: You can use these sections in any order you wish (e.g., you might want to use **Digging Deeper III**, but not **Digging Deeper I** or **Digging Deeper II**).

6. Prepare your classroom ahead of time, setting up and testing an overhead projector and screen and a VCR. If you plan to hand out biblical references for students to look up and read aloud, prepare 3x5 cards (one reference per card) to distribute before class.

Lesson Plan

Step One: "Lachish"

1. Introduction: The Siege of Lachish

Imagine that you and your family are trapped in the ancient city of Lachish as it is besieged by one of the cruelest armies the world has ever known—the army of Assyria. Though the city walls are strong, you and your fellow citizens are vastly outnumbered by the enemy soldiers outside. Your only hope is your own royal army in the mountains 40 miles away. Every day, you turn your eyes to the hills and wonder when help will arrive. You review the events that led to this terrible situation and ask, "How could God let this happen? Could it have been prevented? Is there any hope? Has God forsaken us?"

As explorers of the ruins of ancient Israel, we will seek answers to these questions. To be able to apply the Bible's record to our lives, we will need to understand the history of Lachish and its people. In some ways, we live in Lachish today. Not our city walls, but our values are besieged by powerful societal forces. We also can ask, "How did we get here? Could we have prevented this situation? Where will we go from here? Has God forsaken us?"

As we begin this lesson, encourage your students to recognize that as Christians, they too are under attack. Think of an example where secular society seeks to destroy God's values, and discuss this briefly with the class. Encourage your students to think of similar examples. In this frame of reference, the study of Lachish will be relevant to their struggle to be strong witnesses to God today.

2. Map Study: The Middle Eastern World and Israel

HINT: *Begin this map study session by reviewing the geography of the overall area and working down to the area the lesson is dealing with—Lachish.*

Using the overhead transparency "The Middle Eastern World," point out the following areas, and have your students find them on their maps.

> Assyria
> Israel
> Egypt
> the international trade route (Via Maris)

Using the overhead transparency "Topography of Israel," point out the following areas, and have your students find them on their maps.

> the coastal plain
> the Shephelah
> the Negev
> the Great Rift Valley (Jordan River, Dead Sea, Sea of Galilee)
> the central mountain range (Hebron Mountains)

Using the overhead transparency "Israel," point out the following cities, and have your students find them on their maps.

Samaria   Gezer
Jerusalem   Lachish
Hebron

3. Review the Overhead Transparency "Chronology of Bible Times"

Using the overhead transparency "Chronology of Bible Times," highlight the following dates for your students:

1000 B.C.	David, Solomon
900 B.C.	Kingdom divides
	Jeroboam, Rehoboam, Omri, Ahab, Jezebel, Elijah, Elisha, Jehoshaphat
800 B.C.	Jeroboam II (Amos, Hosea, ca. 750), Joash
700 B.C.	Hezekiah, Isaiah
	Assyria destroys Samaria (north), Sennacherib attacks Judah (south)
600 B.C.	Josiah, Jeremiah
586 B.C.	Judah falls to Babylonians, people are carried into captivity

4. Show the Video *The Wages of Sin* (24 minutes)

5. Guided Discussion: Guarding the Approaches to Jerusalem

The Israelites lived primarily in the central mountains, and after David became king, he made Jerusalem the center of their religion, and even their national identity. It was crucial, therefore, that the city not fall into enemy hands. To protect Jerusalem, the outposts guarding the approaches to it at the edge of the mountains—the key cities of Micmash, Gezer, Beth Shemesh, Azekah, and Lachish—had to be controlled.

Ask students to look up the following passages and note the approaches to Jerusalem.

- 1 Samuel 13:23–14:1,11–15—the ascent to Beth Horon, guarded by Micmash on the east and Gezer on the west.

- Judges 13–16—the Soreq Valley, guarded by Beth Shemesh. (Samson's task was to defend Israel from the Philistines in the Soreq Valley.) Note especially Judges 13:24–25 (the Soreq is just below Zorah and Eshtaol) and 16:4–5 (the Philistines lived in the Soreq).

- 1 Samuel 17:1–3,52—the Elah Valley, guarded by Azekah.

- Isaiah 36:1–2—Wadi Lachish (which enters the Hebron Mountains toward Jerusalem from the south), guarded by Lachish.

Have your students briefly discuss their summaries. NOTE: God's earthly presence was in the mountains in the temple at Jerusalem. It was also where the king lived and where the Israelite army was headquartered. The Hebrew believer naturally would turn to Jerusalem when he needed help from his government or when he sought God. Have a student read Psalm 121:1–2 aloud.

Ask your students to answer the following questions:

a. Why are each of the battles described in the passages above important to Israel's survival? Why did they happen where they did?

b. Why is Jerusalem so important?

c. Where was Jerusalem? Where was its defense line?

d. Why would this prayer in Psalm 121 make geographic sense to an Israelite? NOTE: Help was not in the hills but in God who dwells in the hills.

The geographic principle that the city of Jerusalem must be defended at the outposts illustrates a spiritual truth. Protecting the core of our Christian faith is important. But our defense of our faith begins by defending our values on minor issues first. By the time the foundation of our faith is under attack, we have lost all strategic advantage. We've allowed the enemy to pass unscathed by the outposts defending the approaches to our "Jerusalem."

Viewing sexually explicit movies and television shows in our society, for example, is a serious but indirect threat to the existence of Christian values. It is a Lachish—an outpost defense point. If not stopped at the outpost, however, this practice does lead to moral decay and the decline of the family in our society. This now becomes a direct threat to the value system of the Christian faith—our Jerusalem. Living for God means that we defend His values wherever and whenever they are under attack, on major and minor issues.

Have your students (individually or in small groups) complete the following statements:

a. The "Jerusalems" (key beliefs and values) of the Christian faith are_____

_____.

b. The "Lachishs" (less-central issues that may not seem important but must be defended to protect more-crucial values) are_____

_____.

Ask your students if they can remember a compromise they made on a "minor" issue that led to compromise on a more significant issue. If they feel comfortable doing so, they should relate their experiences to the class.

HINT: *If you have Set 1 of this curriculum, it would be helpful to review with your students the section on city gates (Step 2 in Lesson 1).*

OPTIONAL — Digging Deeper I: Why Are *Tels* Important? *(10–15 minutes)*

(HINT: *If you have Set 1 of this curriculum and the optional overhead-transparency packet, you might want to review Lesson 4's* **Digging Deeper I** *on Israel's tels.*)

Have your students re-read the handout "How to Tell a *Tel*" in Lesson 6.

A. Lecture: Tel Lachish

The setting of this lesson is the *tel* of Lachish. This city was first settled more than 4,000 years before Jesus. It was destroyed and rebuilt at least six times, with each settlement building upon the last. Between these total destructions, several changes in civilization occurred. For example, the layer of Hezekiah's time (700 B.C.) contains massive fortification towers, a huge gate complex, and a palace. Another layer contains the remains of the fiery destruction of this city (587 B.C.).

Tels like Lachish are found throughout Israel. Many of them were old even before Abraham walked the land. All contain a record of the peoples who lived there, including the people of the Bible. Discovering and interpreting the archaeological record from these *tels* can provide insight into God's Word.

B. Personal Application

Ask your students to look up the following passages and respond to the questions:

- Joshua 11:12–13
- Jeremiah 30:18
- Jeremiah 49:2

  1. What is the value of a *tel* for a contemporary Christian?
  2. Do we need to "prove" the Bible? Why or why not? NOTE: We trust the Bible because it is God's Word, not because we can prove it. Archaeological excavation of *tels* provides us with insights into ancient times that help us interpret and better understand the message of the Bible.

6. Guided Discussion: The Israelites' Descent into Evil

HINT: *Your students might find it helpful to review the handout "The Fertility Cults of Canaan" in Lesson 6 before beginning this section.*

Ask students to read aloud the following passages and note the Israelites' descent into paganism:

ISRAEL

a. 1 Kings 11:4–8
b. 1 Kings 12:26–30 (Reminder: Baal worship was connected with the symbol of a bull or calf, so this was a first official step toward paganism for the nation of Israel. See 1 Kings 18:22–24.)
c. 1 Kings 16:25–26
d. 1 Kings 16:29–33

JUDAH

a. 1 Kings 14:22–24
b. 2 Chronicles 28:1–4
c. 2 Chronicles 33:1–6

Have your students respond (individually or in small groups) to the following questions:

1. What do these passages tell us about Israel? About God?
2. Why didn't those who were faithful to God do anything about the terrible practices taking place in their culture?
3. Why doesn't the Christian community today have a greater impact on ungodly trends in our society?
4. The Christian community is made up of individuals. How could you as a Christian be a more positive influence in your community?

Israel and Judah's descent into unfaithfulness began with small steps. Over time, the people's commitment to Baal became nearly complete. By then it was too late for them to avoid God's judgment. Will we learn from their experience?

* * * * * * * * *

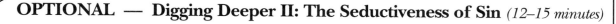

OPTIONAL — Digging Deeper II: The Seductiveness of Sin *(12–15 minutes)*

A. Lecture: The Evils of Baal/Asherah Worship

God's people struggled against the seductiveness of paganism. Soon after entering the Promised Land, they began worshiping Canaan's gods, Baal and Asherah. Worship of these gods involved two particularly evil practices: human sacrifice and ritual sexual perversion. Scholars are divided about the extent and nature of child sacrifice practiced by the Baal cult. The Bible clearly states that it happened, and the number of references to it probably indicates that it was widely practiced at certain times in Israel's history. The worship of Asherah, a significant part of the Canaanite fertility cults, apparently involved various types of sexual perversion, including religious prostitution.

B. Guided Discussion

Before beginning this section, review Guided Discussions 3 and 6 under Step 2 in Lesson 6. Then ask students to respond to the following questions:

1. Why are child sacrifice and ritual sexual perversion particularly evil?

2. What specific symbols or rituals were used in the worship of Asherah?

3. How could God's people have been caught up in these horrible practices? (There are many reasons for their adoption. Be sure to include the role of Israel's kings in promoting the cult.)

4. What are the obvious similarities between Baal worship and our culture today?

5. How did we, as a civilization, get caught in these evil practices?

Lead students in a few moments of prayer. Ask them to pray specifically about the sexual immorality and destruction of innocent life in our culture.

Step Two: "God's Judgment and Hezekiah's Faith"

1. Lecture: God Is Faithful

God's patience with His people, even in the face of their repeated rebellion, is incredible. The Israelites bowed down to idols and sacrificed their children to them. They practiced sorcery and divination, and they prostituted themselves in the name of religion. Yet God remained faithful and continued to call them back to Himself. Through His prophets, He repeatedly warned the Israelites that they would be punished for their sins (Deuteronomy 8:10–14 and 28:15,49–52; Jeremiah 1:14–16; Hosea 10:1–8), but they ignored Him. Finally, God had had enough. He sent the cruelest army the world has ever known, the Assyrians, to ravage Israel and carry its people into exile.

2. Guided Discussion: God Used the Assyrians to Judge His People

Your students should read 2 Kings 17 and the handout "The Palace of a Great King." Then ask them to read the following passages and respond to the questions:

*   2 Kings 17:5–6. What was the form of God's judgment? What did you learn about the Assyrian army from the video and the handout?

*   2 Kings 17:7–11,16–17. What was Israel's sin? What particular sins finally brought God's severest judgment?

- 2 Kings 17:12. How could the Israelites have known this? (See Exodus 23:13; Leviticus 26:1; Deuteronomy 5:6–10.) (**HINT:** *Point your students to Leviticus 18 [especially verses 24–28], which lists all forbidden sexual perversions and the warning that if the Israelites practiced these perversions, they would lose the land God promised them. Also, note the contemporary character of the sins.*) Why were the Israelites so blind? How could our culture know the nature of our sin and God's anger? What can you do to identify the evil of our culture and to present that truth to others? Why are we so blind?

- 2 Kings 17:13. Did God judge the Israelites immediately? (Note Amos 3:12 and 6:1–7. Amos wrote many years before these prophecies occurred.) Does God judge us immediately? Who are our prophets? What can you do to be a prophet? List several items, and discuss them with the class.

- 2 Kings 17:18–20,23. God's judgment was final at this point. The northern 10 tribes never returned to Israel. They have been lost to history. When God reaches the end of His patience, there is no turning back. Has God's judgment begun against our culture? If yes, what are the signs that it has started? Is it too late to stop it?

- What other biblical examples show God's seemingly endless patience and mercy dramatically turned into judgment on evil? (For example, the Flood in Genesis 6–9 and Sodom and Gomorrah in Genesis 19.)

In Lesson 10, we investigate Arad, a small city not far from Lachish that was also destroyed by the Assyrians. Arad is a fascinating study because there is no sign of Baal worship there. Archaeologists found much evidence of the worship of Yahweh, including a temple similar in style and design to the tabernacle and Solomon's temple. Clearly, Arad was a town of God-fearing people who did not participate in the pagan practices of the rest of the country. Yet these people died horribly at the hands of the same brutal army that destroyed Lachish.

Ask your students to respond to the following questions:

- When God judges a culture, can anyone hope to escape because they didn't participate in the sins?

- What does this mean for the responsibility of the faithful before God's judgment comes?

- How would you apply this concept to our culture? What is your responsibility to your culture?

3. Guided Discussion: God's Terrible Justice

a. *Preparation*

Before beginning this section, prepare Overhead Transparency 9 ("The Siege of Lachish") for viewing.

b. *Lecture: The Assyrian Army*

The Assyrian army was one of the most brutal armies the world has ever known. The Assyrians believed in inflicting maximum suffering on their enemies as a way of intimidating anyone who might resist them. Few survived their onslaught. Individuals with certain skills or abilities (e.g., those who could write) might be spared. All others died horrible deaths.

Assyrian kings took great pride in recording their military conquests in writing (on tablets, clay cylinders, and obelisks) and in pictorial reliefs on stone slabs lining palace walls. Along with a recounting of victories won and plunder taken are chilling lists of how their captives were tortured. These included:

- flaying (cutting skin into strips and pulling it off a living victim)
- beheading

- impaling (inserting a sharpened stake beneath the rib cage of a living victim, putting the stake in the ground so it stood erect, and leaving the victim hanging on it until it pierced a vital organ)

- burning captives (especially young victims) alive

- severing hands and feet

- gouging out eyes

- severing noses, ears, tongues, and testicles

Though we would consider this list obscene, it is important for us to realize two things:

1. God's anger at idolatry, particularly the shedding of innocent blood, is fierce. His use of the Assyrians to punish His people can be understood only in light of the evil of Baal worship. The heinousness of Israel's sin is evidenced by the dreadfulness of the punishment.

2. When God finally judges sin, His justice is terrible. NOTE: Point your students to the Last Judgment, where God's righteousness will again be demonstrated against unrepentant sinners (Matthew 24:45–51).

OPTIONAL — Digging Deeper III: Judah's Four Good Kings
(33–50 minutes)

A. Lecture: The Kings of Judah

The northern tribes (Israel) were destroyed in 722 B.C. God's patience had finally run out, and these people would never again exist as a nation. The southern tribes (Judah) continued for more than a century before they too fell to God's judgment, this time at the hands of the Babylonians and their king Nebuchadnezzar. Why did Judah survive so much longer than Israel? Part of the reason God gave the southern tribes more time to repent was His promise to David that his kingdom would endure forever (2 Samuel 7:16). Also, Judah was blessed with several God-fearing, faithful kings who brought the people back—at least temporarily—from the brink of disaster.

B. Guided Discussion: Influencing Society for Good

Divide the class into small groups, and assign each group a king of Judah to research. The following items should be summarized for each king:

- the spiritual condition of Judah at the time of the king's reign

- the specific actions the king took to reestablish a relationship with God

- the specific actions the king took to confront evil

- the blessings of God that followed (either the writer's commendation of the king or specific conditions that resulted from the king's obedience to God)

Group 1. King Asa—2 Chronicles 14–16

Group 2. King Joash—2 Chronicles 22:10–12 and 24:1–27 (note his disobedience later in life)

Group 3. King Hezekiah—2 Chronicles 29–32

Group 4. King Josiah—2 Chronicles 34–35

Have each group give a summary of its findings. Then ask the students if there is a pattern to each situation. Reflect on the following as a class:

1. What part did these four kings have in God's sparing Judah?

2. What was the relationship between their faith and their actions?

3. Who today would fit a similar description (i.e., devoted to God and ready to confront evil in a godly way)?

4. What can we, as Christians, learn from these four kings that we can apply in our culture?

Spend a few moments in prayer, asking God to teach us to be obedient and to use our influence on family and society to bring about spiritual and moral reform.

4. Guided Discussion: Hezekiah's Religious Reforms

a. *Preparation*

Before beginning this section, set up Overhead Transparency 10 ("Destruction of the High Places") for viewing.

b. *Guided Discussion: Hezekiah's Role in God's Judgment on the Israelites*

King Hezekiah played a key role in God's judgment on Israel and Judah for their Baal worship, particularly child sacrifice and sexual perversion (2 Kings 17:16–17). Ask your students to look up the passages listed below to see his part in this drama.

- 2 Chronicles 29:1–2—Hezekiah was a good king.

- 2 Chronicles 29:6–8—He understood the spiritual nature of the problem.

- 2 Chronicles 29:20–24,27—He restored the people's relationship with Yahweh.

- 2 Chronicles 31:1—The pagans' shrines were demolished and their values rejected.

    A typical high place, with the Baal figure and an Asherah pole, is shown in Overhead Transparency 10. These places were sources of sin in Israel's life. Hezekiah was 25 years old when he became king of Judah. Totally devoted to God, he undertook one of the greatest religious reforms the nation of Israel had ever seen. He repaired the temple in Jerusalem and restored worship services. Under his direction, the Israelites destroyed all the high places, Asherah poles, and sacred stones they had set up to Baal. Because the people kept returning to pagan practices, such total destruction was necessary. It is important to recognize that the same principle applies to us. To follow God faithfully, we must be willing to destroy our "high places" (sinful practices, habits, and "gods" to which we are devoted).

    Ask each student to identify a high place in his or her own life. How might it be destroyed? If they are willing, students may give their examples to the class.

    Stop for a moment to pray. If some students have related their personal "high places," pray for them specifically. Pray for all the students in their battles against sin.

- 2 Chronicles 31:21—God blessed the people because they were faithful.

- 2 Chronicles 32:1—God's judgment on the culture still arrived.

- 2 Chronicles 32:2–8—Hezekiah prepared as well as he could to defend God's people against the threat. He brought about spiritual renewal, destroying pagan altars and practices. Now he prepared the people to confront the Assyrian army. Notice the result in verse 8.

    Can you think of anyone in your experience who has been a "Hezekiah" for others? Have you ever helped others "gain confidence"?

- 2 Chronicles 32:9–19—While at Lachish (verse 9), Sennacherib, the king of the Assyrians, challenged Hezekiah and his God. He mocked what Hezekiah had done (verse 12), ridiculed the faith of the people (verses 14–15), and wrote a threatening letter to Hezekiah (see also Isaiah 36:1–22).

  Can you think of a similar situation in our day where someone challenged the beliefs of God's people, mocked what we have done, and ridiculed our faith in God's ability to provide a solution?

- Isaiah 37:1,14–20—Hezekiah turned the matter over to the Lord. Note that his prayer acknowledged the greatness of God (verse 16) and stated his motive: ". . . so that all kingdoms on earth may know that you alone, O Lord, are God" (verse 20). This is what motivates those who serve God. They act so others may see God through them. That should be our motivation, too.

- Isaiah 37:21,33–35—God responded because of Hezekiah's faith.

- Isaiah 37:36—God's anger at those who threaten His people and who mock Him is severe. His destruction of 185,000 Assyrian soldiers in their camp outside Jerusalem weakened the army so much that Assyria fell to Babylon soon after.

c. *Personal Application*

Your students should consider the implications of Israel's history for our culture. Ask them to respond to the following questions:

1. What were the steps Hezekiah took to confront evil? In what ways do they apply to us?

2. What could you do to restore your relationship with God? With others?

3. Choose one evil our culture faces. What can we do to destroy it? Has everything possible been done? What could you do to help? Can we trust God to bring the results He desires if we lay the matter before Him? How would you lay this before God?

4. What was Hezekiah's motive in confronting evil (Isaiah 37:18–20)?

* * * * * * * * * *

OPTIONAL — Digging Deeper IV: Hezekiah's Water System
(15–20 minutes)

(This section requires the use of the optional full-color overhead-transparency packet. If you need information on ordering it, see inside front cover.)

A. Lecture

The main water supply for the city of Jerusalem was the spring of Gihon, which flowed out of a cave on the eastern side of the hill on which the city stood. The Hebrew word means "gushing out" and was given because the spring does not have a steady flow but bursts from the rock at various times each day. Before David captured Jerusalem about 1000 B.C., the Jebusite inhabitants dug a shaft from the city into the cave. Thereafter, they were able to draw water from the pool below.

The entrance to the cave was outside Jerusalem's walls, in the Kidron Valley. This was a significant weakness in the city's defense because the water supply was exposed to enemies. In fact, it is possible that Joab, David's commander, entered the cave and climbed up the shaft to capture the city for David (2 Samuel 5:8; 1 Chronicles 11:6).

When King Hezekiah learned that the dreaded Assyrian army had arrived in Israel, he recognized the threat his exposed water supply posed for Jerusalem's survival. He dug a tunnel through the ridge on which the city was built, bringing water to the other side, and then covered up the cave's opening (2 Kings 20:20; 2 Chronicles 32:2–4). (The walled part of Jerusalem was at a lower elevation on the western side of the ridge, so the water could flow to a pool, the pool of Siloam, within the city walls.) To this day, this extraordinary accomplishment ranks as one of the engineering marvels of the ancient world.

B. Visual Insights

The following overhead transparencies are of Hezekiah's tunnel.

Overhead Transparency 22. The Cave of the Spring of Gihon. The water flowing out of this cave, the source of the spring of Gihon, is the reason Jerusalem was built on the ridge above. The spring provides more than 34,250 cubic feet of water per day. The water runs from the cave a short distance (about 33 feet) to a water chamber. Above the water chamber, a shaft was dug 37 feet up to a tunnel. The tunnel continues another 65 feet to a vaulted entrance just inside the city walls. People in the city would enter the upper tunnel and walk to the top of the shaft. From here they could lower their containers to the water chamber below. The chamber could not handle the volume of water from the spring, so most of it drained into the Kidron Valley, where it was channeled along the base of the ridge for irrigation and other purposes.

Overhead Transparency 23. Hezekiah's Water Tunnel. This tunnel was created by Hezekiah's workmen more than 700 years before Jesus. Working from the spring of Gihon on one side and the western slope of the ridge of Jerusalem on the other, two teams of workmen created a tunnel by chiseling through solid rock, at points more than 140 feet underground. The tunnel is 1,748 feet long and follows a circuitous path. The distance in a straight line between the spring and the pool of Siloam, where it empties, is slightly more than 1,000 feet. The winding course of the tunnel adds more than 700 feet to its length. How these two teams chiseled a tunnel barely two feet wide, with a drop of just 12 inches in the quarter-mile length, to meet in the middle amazes even modern engineers. Some speculate that workers followed natural cracks in the rock or seeping water. However it was done, the result helped save the city of Jerusalem from the Assyrian siege.

When visiting Jerusalem, modern students of Bible history often choose to walk through Hezekiah's tunnel. Still today water flows through it more than waist deep. At some points, an adult must bend over because the ceiling is so low, and at many places the tunnel is so narrow that both shoulders rub the walls. The chisel marks left on the walls by the workers as they dug through the rock are a silent testimony to the vision and determination of the Israelite people.

The tunnel is evidence of Hezekiah's resolve to do everything possible to prepare his people to face the Assyrians. Though he trusted God totally (Isaiah 37:14–20), he made sure he had done all he could, including undertaking a project as astounding as this tunnel. That should be the approach of every follower of Yahweh who is called to confront evil. If we would trust God as much as Hezekiah did, and expend the same effort and display his vision, we as a Christian community could make a significant impact in the struggle to promote God's values in our world.

Overhead Transparency 24. The Midway Point in Hezekiah's Tunnel Where the Workers Met. Here is the spot where the tunnelers met nearly at midpoint. The ability of these people to cut this small tunnel without modern instruments or tools is astonishing. The fact that they were only 10 feet off horizontally and none at all vertically appears almost miraculous. Is it possible that God's hand was in the project as well? Given Hezekiah's faith and his trust in God, it seems to be the best explanation.

In 1880, not far from here, several boys playing in the tunnel discovered writing chiseled in the ceiling. Called the Siloam Inscription, it describes the dramatic moment when the two teams of workers met. Scholars have noted that it is one of the few texts memorializing a great event from the perspective of the common people who accomplished it. One translation of the inscription reads: "While the laborers were still working with their picks, each toward the other, and while there were still three cubits to be broken through, the voice of each was heard calling to the other, because there was a split in the rock to the south and to the north. And at the moment of the breakthrough the laborers struck each toward the other, pick against pick. Then the water flowed from the spring to the pool for 1200 cubits. And the height of the rock above the heads of the laborers was 100 cubits." [1] The writer obviously was familiar with the event and with the tunnel. Maybe it was the overseer of the project, or maybe a worker. Whoever the writer was, he recorded an amazing achievement.

Unfortunately, the inscription was taken to Istanbul during the Turkish rule of Palestine in the late nineteenth century and is now in the Istanbul Archaeological Museum. It appears another miracle is needed to return it to its original home—Jerusalem, the city of David and Hezekiah.

5. Guided Discussion: The Evil Manasseh

Ask your students to read the handout "70 Reasons for 70 Years." Then have them (individually or in small groups) read the following passages and answer the questions.

- 2 Chronicles 33:2–6.

    1. What are some of the factors that might have contributed to Hezekiah's son being so evil?

    2. After such a close call with the Assyrians and such a miraculous delivery (Isaiah 37:36–37), how could the people so soon return to evil?

    3. Have you ever been really convicted about a sin in your life, only to return to it soon after? How should a Christian respond to this problem? (See Isaiah 1:15–19.)

- 2 Chronicles 36:5,9,11–12.

    1. What was the nature of most of the kings after Hezekiah?

- 2 Chronicles 36:7,17,20–21.

    1. What was the form of God's judgment on Judah? How was it different from that on Israel?

    2. Why were the people in captivity for *70* years? What does this tell you about God's purposes? How would you apply His concern for the land to us today?

6. Guided Discussion: God's Salvation

a. *Lecture*

It is amazing that Yahweh used sinful human beings to bring about the coming of the Messiah. Both Abraham and David sinned and showed their lack of faith, but Abraham became the father of God's people, and David was a direct ancestor of Jesus. Each of these men had a crucial role in the coming of the Messiah. Salvation is entirely God's doing, yet He chose to use imperfect people to bring it about. As these people acted faithfully, they contributed to God's great work.

b. *Guided Discussion*

Ask your students to read the following passages and answer the questions.

- 2 Kings 17:18–23. What happened to the people of Israel during Hezekiah's reign?

- Isaiah 36:12–15. What did Sennacherib, the king of the Assyrians, suggest would happen to Judah?

- Hebrews 7:14. From a human perspective, what would have happened if Judah had been destroyed?

- Isaiah 37:21. Why did God spare Judah?

c. *Personal Application*

Is it possible for God to use your faithfulness to provide a blessing for people even hundreds of years later? Reflect on God's desire to use you as part of His purpose. Think about what would prevent you from being used by God. Then spend a few moments thanking God for Hezekiah's faithfulness and God's use of this devout king to preserve the salvation plan that has come down through the ages and of which we can be a part.

Conclusion

There are two main points to this lesson. First, the wages of sin remind us that God's judgment will certainly fall on wrongdoing. For centuries, the Israelites persisted in their sin of idol worship, even though God kept calling them back to Himself. Finally, God ran out of patience and sent the dreaded Assyrians to punish His people. Unlike the Israelites, we've been redeemed by Christ's atoning blood. But we are no less accountable for our sinful behavior. If we remain unrepentant, God's judgment will fall upon us as well.

The second point of this lesson is that the wages of sin serve as a challenge to us to be faithful as Hezekiah was faithful. This great king combined human effort with trust in God to prepare the people of Jerusalem to fight against their enemy. Hezekiah's method was threefold. First, he instituted extensive religious reforms in Israel, destroying the high places and other elements of paganism. Second, he built an amazing water system that protected Jerusalem's water supply from attack, making the city less vulnerable to siege. And third, after doing everything he could humanly do, he trusted in God by turning the battle against Assyria over to Him. If we are to be faithful servants of Yahweh, we must follow Hezekiah's example.

Ask your students to write down one area of conflict they find themselves in on God's behalf (e.g., personal habits, practices of friends or colleagues). What specific actions could they take to be like Hezekiah?

After discussing a few of the students' responses, spend some time in prayer, turning over to God their struggles against sin and the secular values of the culture. Ask God to give each person the courage and devotion he or she needs to be like Hezekiah.

Notes

1. Simon B. Parker, "Siloam Inscription Memorializes Engineering Achievement," *Biblical Archaeology Review* (July/Aug. 1994): 37.

THE PALACE OF A GREAT KING

THE ASSYRIAN EMPIRE

Assyria, located in Mesopotamia near the Euphrates River, was one of the great empires of the ancient world. Its history parallels much of the Old Testament. Known for their ruthlessness in battle and horrific treatment of captives, the Assyrians were hated and feared. Their vast armies were equipped with the latest weaponry (e.g., barbed arrows and catapults) and siege machines. No wonder Jonah fled when God commanded him to preach to Nineveh, Assyria's capital (Jonah 1:1–3). God's use of this implacable foe to punish the Israelites for their idol worship, child sacrifice, and sexual perversion underscores His anger against the sins of His people (2 Kings 17:16–18).

ISRAEL IS DESTROYED

The Assyrian king Tiglath-Pileser began plundering Israel in approximately 740 B.C. (2 Kings 15:29). He destroyed many cities, brutally killing the inhabitants, and left Israel with only the capital of Samaria intact. A few years later, Hoshea, the last king of Israel, unwisely refused to pay tribute to the Assyrians. King Shalmaneser marched on Samaria, slaughtered the inhabitants, and destroyed what was left of the northern kingdom. In 722 B.C., these 10 tribes ceased to exist as a people. God's mercy had run out and His judgment was final. The Israelites who remained were forcibly mixed with other religious and ethnic groups and became the hated Samaritans of the New Testament. Those who were deported disappeared from history, though many people believe God was already planning for a future Pentecost (see Acts 2:8–11) and a missionary army to spread the gospel.

SENNACHERIB INVADES JUDAH

After Israel's destruction, the nation of Judah continued a tenuous existence. When would the Assyrian hordes return? How could they hope to escape? Judah's king Hezekiah, recognizing that God was the only possible deliverance, frantically instituted religious reforms. Then, around 700 B.C., the new Assyrian king, Sennacherib, turned his attention to the Israelites. Destroying many cities on his march, he invaded Judah, where Hezekiah had made extensive preparations. Sennacherib's own claim that he destroyed 46 walled cities in Judah and deported over 200,000 captives gives evidence of the massive destruction he wrought. Written on clay tablets and cylinders, these ancient records provide a graphic backdrop to the stories of the Bible.

SENNACHERIB'S PALACE

Assyria's kings were committed to more than military conquest. Part of the religious duty of these monarchs was the construction of massive public buildings. Sennacherib's contribution was a new palace he called the Palace without a Rival. His own records indicate that the labor force that built it was composed of deportees of many conquered nations, probably including Israel.

Archaeologists discovered this magnificent palace in the late nineteenth century. It contains more than 70 halls and chambers, all lined with stone panels (called reliefs) depicting Sennacherib's accomplishments. Enormous statues of winged bulls guard the doors of the hallway to the main chamber. The hallway walls are lined with panels commemorating the destruction of the cities of Judah, including the siege of Lachish.

The panels have a chilling effect on those who have read the Bible's account of Sennacherib's war against Judah. People are shown being flayed alive, while others are having their tongues sliced off. Piles of heads surround the king. On the panel that portrays the taking of the city gate, prisoners are being impaled on stakes outside the city walls in full view of their fellow Israelites. Long lines of prisoners are being led away. Assyrian slingers and siege machines highlight the invincible force Sennacherib brought against Judah.

GOD DESTROYS THE ASSYRIAN ARMY

Clearly, God's people faced great suffering because of their sins. Their very existence hung in the balance. Sennacherib's account of the battle of Jerusalem reveals how desperate the situation was. He bragged that he had made Hezekiah a prisoner, "like a bird in a cage." But this proud, cruel king failed to give the whole story. Sennacherib's blasphemous attitude and his attack on the faithful people of Judah were beyond what God would bear. According to the Bible, the angel of the Lord came to the Assyrian camp and killed 185,000 soldiers in one night, forcing the army to retreat. Soon after, the Assyrian empire went into decline.

HEZEKIAH'S FAITH SAVED JUDAH

Although the Israelites deserved to be punished, God delivered them because of Hezekiah's faith and trust in Him (Isaiah 37:14–21,36). Hezekiah did what he could to prepare Jerusalem against attack, but his ultimate trust was in God, not himself. Today we must have Hezekiah's faith to combat the evils of secular society. God wants us to use the means at our disposal to fight against our enemies. But He also wants us to realize that our survival is in His hands. If we place our trust in our own strength, we are lost. Only God can win the battle.

70 REASONS FOR 70 YEARS

THE EXILE

The Judgment

The Israelites' continued disobedience finally brought God to the end of His patience. Judgment came when the people of Israel (the northern 10 tribes) were destroyed by the Assyrians in 722 B.C. and when the people of Judah were exiled to Babylon in 586 B.C. The writer of Kings, living at the time of these disasters, saw the link between Israel's continued participation in the cult of Baal and the judgment of exile (2 Kings 17:18–19). The author of Chronicles, writing after Israel's return from captivity, portrayed the fall of Jerusalem and the destruction of the temple as resulting from the people's sins (2 Chronicles 36:15–19).

Hope in Disaster

The biblical reality of a God who hates sin and will eventually punish it—reinforced in the stories of the Flood, Sodom and Gomorrah, the conquest of Canaan, and now the exile to Babylon—is one with significant implications for our time. But the writer of Chronicles also saw hope in disaster. God did not forsake His own, nor did He end His plan for the redemption of His people. Second Chronicles 36:22–23 ends with optimism, because the Israelites will return to their land. The question remained, however: Would they (and we) learn from the disaster?

THE CAPTIVITY

The Babylonian Captivity (586 B.C.) was in many ways a time of spiritual growth for God's people. Without their temple, the Israelites learned that obedience is better than sacrifice (Psalm 40:6; Isaiah 1:10–19). They returned from Babylon focused on God and the need to be faithful to Him (Ezra 10:1-4). Never again would the worship of Baal and the shedding of innocent blood be the religion of the nation.

Israel learned another lesson during its captivity. God taught His people the importance of obeying all of His commands or suffering the consequences. In the process, God demonstrated to them the respect they must have for the land He entrusted to them because it is His creation.

WHY 70 YEARS?

Students of the Bible know that the Babylonian Captivity, as God's judgment on Israel's sin, lasted for 70 years. Rarely is the question asked, "Why 70?" Second Chronicles 36:21 gives us the answer.

The Sabbath Principle

God made the sabbath principle a central one in His creation. To recognize God's ownership of everything, the seventh day is set apart (made holy) to the Lord. Violating the Sabbath day is a serious sin because it denies God's sovereignty. This concept was so important that God applied it to the creation itself. Every seventh year, the land was to lie fallow. The Israelites were not to sow or prune or reap. Whatever grew of its own accord could be eaten, but the land was not to be farmed. As a symbol of God's ownership, it was to rest (Leviticus 25:1–7). Yahweh promised an abundant crop in the sixth year, so no one would go hungry during the following sabbath year (Leviticus 25:20–22).

Idolatry Does Not Recognize God's Sovereignty

One reason Yahweh condemned idolatry is that it did not acknowledge Him as the one true God. Idol worshipers worked on the Sabbath day (Jeremiah 17:19–27; Isaiah 58:13) because they did not recognize that they belonged to God. They worked the land in the seventh year because they denied Yahweh's ownership of it. God warned Israel that this is where idol worship would lead. In Leviticus 26, God told the Israelites that if they continued to be disobedient, their land would be taken from them so that it "will have the rest it did not have during the sabbaths you lived in it" (verse 35).

God Punishes the Israelites for Their Idolatry

Since the Israelites' illicit affair with pagan gods began almost as soon as they arrived in Canaan, it's unlikely they obeyed the sabbath principle, especially in regard to the land. God's ownership was not considered significant. But God demands obedience. Soon He ripped His stiff-necked people from their land, giving it back the sabbath and asserting His ownership over it and them (2 Chronicles 36:21).

The Meaning of the 70 Years

Scholars debate whether, by the time of their captivity, the Israelites had been in the Promised Land for 70 sabbath years (meaning one for every seven years, or 490 years), or whether the number 70 indicated 10 (completeness) sevens (sabbaths). Whatever the case, God essentially said, "If you will not recognize My ownership and give the land its rest, I will do it Myself, for it is that important to Me." So the Israelites had to leave, and the land rested for the 70 years it had coming. How the people must have wished they had recognized God's ownership and kept His sabbaths!

CONCLUSION

Like Israel, Western culture has systematically eliminated signs of God's ownership. For example, many believe religion is now a personal affair and should never be considered in politics, education, or law; today the Ten Commandments cannot be publicly displayed and do not play a role in public life; and morality is now subjective—that is, there is no ultimate source of right and wrong. The false gods of secular humanism have stripped the marks of Yahweh's ownership from much of what is rightfully His.

The lesson of Israel's 70 years of exile is clear. God will punish sin. And He will restore all things to Himself because they are already His. The question is, will we who know God as Lord of heaven and earth act to reestablish His claims on our society before it is too late?

THE LORD IS MY SHEPHERD

For the Teacher

The Bible was written by people who were part of a culture very different from our own. They were Eastern in their way of thinking, and we, of course, are Western. We might say the Bible writers were "Hebrew" thinkers, while we are "Greek" thinkers. Although it is difficult to state simply the contrast between ancient Near Eastern thinking and our own, one key difference is our tendency to use abstract definitions and the Israelites' preference for concrete examples. Where we might define God as omnipotent and compassionate, the biblical writer would say, "The Lord is my Shepherd," which is one of the most profound and common metaphors used in the Bible to describe God and His relationship to His people: the shepherd and his flock.

The Bible stresses that the heart of godliness is relationship rather than simply intellectual agreement with truth. In this lesson, help your students to see the "pictures" the Bible uses in this context as concrete definitions of relationship. Ask them to develop their own pictures of God from their own experiences. The result will be a God who seems more real and personal than the abstract definitions we often use to describe Him. The Bible comes alive when we remember that the word pictures it uses are true representations of God's nature and our relationship with Him.

Your Objectives for This Lesson

At the completion of this section, you will want your students:

To Know/Understand

1. The character or nature of the wilderness and its significance in the faith of the Israelites.

2. The geography and topography of the Judea Wilderness and the Negev.

3. The events of the Bible that took place in the wilderness.

4. That the forefathers of the Jewish people were wilderness nomads and shepherds.

5. The unique lifestyle of the wilderness shepherd and how the shepherd's relationship with his sheep parallels God's relationship with His people.

To Do

1. Recognize God as their Shepherd and learn to hear and follow His voice in their daily wildernesses.

2. Apply the significance of "quiet waters" and "green pastures" to their own lives.

3. Understand the straight paths God would have them follow.

How to Plan for This Lesson

Because of the volume of material in this lesson, you may need to divide it into several class sessions. To help you determine how to do that, the lesson has been broken into segments that can each be covered in approximately one hour. The end of each of these segments is marked by a row of asterisks.

If, however, you need to cover the entire lesson in one 60-minute session, you should include the following elements in your lesson plan:

- Step One—sections 1, 2 (Negev only), 3, and 4
- Step Two—sections 1, 2, 6, and 7

How to Prepare for This Lesson

Materials Needed

Student copies of the maps: "The Middle Eastern World"
    "Topography of Israel"

Overhead transparencies: "The Middle Eastern World"
    "Topography of Israel"
    "Chronology of Bible Times"

Student copies of the handout: "Not on Bread Alone"

Video: **The Lord Is My Shepherd**

Overhead projector, screen, VCR

1. Make copies of the "Middle Eastern World" and "Topography of Israel" maps for your students.

2. Prepare the overhead transparencies "The Middle Eastern World," "Topography of Israel," and "Chronology of Bible Times."

3. Make copies of the handout "Not on Bread Alone" for your students. (If possible, students should receive and read this handout before the lesson.)

4. Determine which optional **Digging Deeper** sections, if any, you want to use in your class session(s). NOTE: You can use these sections in any order you wish (e.g., you might want to use **Digging Deeper III**, but not **Digging Deeper I** or **Digging Deeper II**).

5. Review the geography of the lands of the Bible from the "Introduction."

6. Prepare your classroom ahead of time, setting up and testing an overhead projector and screen and a VCR. If you plan to hand out biblical references for your students to look up and read aloud, prepare 3x5 cards (one reference per card) to distribute before class.

Lesson Plan

Step One: "The Wilderness"

1. Introductory Comments

When God designed His salvation plan, He determined a time for it to be set in motion, and He selected a people to help carry it out. We often overlook the fact that God also chose a particular location for His saving work. His choice of *where* His plan would take place is as important as *when* and *through whom*.

In this lesson, we will study one region of the land God chose to carry out His plan for humankind: the wilderness. Comprising the Judea Wilderness in eastern Israel and the Negev in southern Israel, the wilderness played a significant role in shaping biblical history and the images and metaphors God used to describe Himself and His relationship with His people. Long after the Hebrews had settled in the more hospitable land of Canaan, their wilderness experience continued to shape their identity. Because the wilderness is the home of nomadic shepherds, it is not surprising that the Israelites saw God as their Shepherd.

2. Map Study: Israel's Wilderness

HINT: *Begin this map study session by reviewing the geography of the overall region and working down to the area the lesson is dealing with—Israel's wilderness.*

Using the overhead transparency "The Middle Eastern World," point out the following areas, and have your students locate them on their maps.

> Mesopotamia (the eastern empires of Assyria, Persia, Babylon)
> Egypt (the western empire)
> the Tigris and Euphrates Rivers
> the Nile River
> the Mediterranean Sea
> the Arabian Desert
> Israel (note its location between the desert and the sea and between the eastern and western empires)

Using the overhead transparency "Topography of Israel," point out the following areas, and have your students locate them on their maps.

the coastal plain	Beersheba
the Negev	the Mediterranean Sea
Jerusalem	Arad
Jericho	
the central mountain range (Hebron Mountains, Judea Mountains, Samaria Mountains)	
the Great Rift Valley (Jordan River, Dead Sea, Sea of Galilee)	

3. Review the Overhead Transparency "Chronology of Bible Times"

Using the overhead transparency "Chronology of Bible Times," highlight the following dates for your students:

1900 B.C.	Abraham goes to Canaan
1400 B.C.	Moses, Exodus
1000 B.C.	David
ca. 6 B.C.	Jesus' birth
ca. A.D. 29	Jesus' death and resurrection, Pentecost

4. View the Video *The Lord Is My Shepherd* (18 minutes)

5. Read the Handout "Not on Bread Alone"

Students should review the Bible passages listed in this handout.

6. Guided Discussion: The Wilderness Experience

In the wilderness, God formed Israel into His people. It was here that they learned to trust God to provide for them, and it was here that God disciplined them and shaped their faith. In later times of trouble, the prophets called for the Israelites to return to the faith of their infancy in the desert (Jeremiah 2:1–8, 9:2, 31:31–32; Psalm 81:1–10; Hosea 2:14–15).

Have your students (individually or in small groups) read the following passages and state the geographical setting of each passage and the significant contribution each person or event made to the formation of God's people:

    a.   Genesis 12:1–9
    b.   Genesis 21:1–7 (note also Genesis 20:1)
    c.   Exodus 3:1–15
    d.   Exodus 20:1–17 (note also Exodus 19:1–2)
    e.   Deuteronomy 2:7 (Moses speaking to the people of Israel)
    f.   1 Samuel 23:14, 24:1, 25:1, 26:2–4

Notice that Israel's forefathers (Abraham, the father of the Israelite nation; Moses, the lawgiver; and David, the founder of the kingdom of Israel) all prepared for the missions God gave them by spending time in the desert (Genesis 12:9; Exodus 3:1; 1 Samuel 24:1).

Later biblical writers understood the desert as the place where God created faith in His people. When they grew hungry, God fed them manna from the sky and quail from the sea. When they complained of thirst, He gave them water from rock. When their fear of the unknown overwhelmed them and they began to curse Moses for leading them out of Egypt, God sent a plague of poisonous snakes as punishment for their unfaithfulness. By nurturing and disciplining His people, God was teaching them to depend solely upon Him. And though the Israelites continued to rebel, God remained faithful. God made His covenant with the Israelites in the wilderness, and their experience there transformed them from a band of people into a powerful nation. Believers must constantly relearn these wilderness lessons.

Ask your students to look up the following passages and note the link between the people of that day and their past wilderness experience.

    a.   Psalm 78:9–16
    b.   Psalm 78:17–32
    c.   Psalm 95:6–11
    d.   Jeremiah 2:1–2
    e.   Deuteronomy 8:1–5,10–18

Ask your students to summarize the lessons Israel learned in the wilderness. Point out that the wilderness was never meant to be the Israelites' permanent home; rather, it was a place of learning to trust the faithfulness of God, and it was the way to the Promised Land. The desert was for them a "conversion" experience, after which they were called to live in obedience to God in His chosen land.

7. Personal Application

Ask your students how they would apply the concept of the wilderness to their own lives. Ask them to reflect on those times or experiences in which they were forced to learn dependence upon God alone.

    a.   How have they been tested?

    b.   Did they see God's gracious provision during these times? If yes, in what ways?

    c.   How did these wilderness times prepare them to live for God?

    d.   Can they recall occasions when they forgot the lessons of these wilderness times?

    e.   How might they relive these experiences to return to a deeper trust in God?

Ask students to relate briefly their wilderness times, if they desire.

* * * * * * * * * *

OPTIONAL — Digging Deeper I: The Wadis of Israel *(15 minutes)*

(This section requires the use of the optional full-color overhead-transparency packet. If you need information on ordering it, see inside front cover.)

A. Lecture

The wilderness of Israel is scarred by riverbeds called wadis (Hebrew: *nahal*). They are formed by rain runoff in the mountains and are often deep and rugged. The life of the shepherd is helped and hindered by these canyons. Water stands in them after a flood, causing shade-producing trees to grow. But crossing them is difficult, and the danger of flash floods during the rainy season is great.

The Bible's water imagery is based partly on the contrast between the barren desert and the lush vegetation that springs up after flash floods crash through these dry canyons, leaving behind quiet pools. The coming of the Messiah is compared to streams in the desert (Isaiah 32:1–2), a reference to the suddenness of His appearance and the life that blossoms afterward.

B. Visual Insights

The following overhead transparencies show the beauty of a variety of wadis in the Judea Wilderness and the Negev.

Overhead Transparency 25. A Wadi in the Negev. In the Middle East, floods in the desert are a frequent occurrence because of the topography of the land. The mountains to the north of the Negev and to the west of the Judea Wilderness get significant amounts of rainfall during the short rainy season. The soil of the mountains cannot absorb this amount of water, so it runs off into the arid wilderness.

This photograph shows the effects of floods in the desert. Though the walls of this wadi are especially steep, the tracks made by rushing water are clearly seen. The wilderness has many of these dry riverbeds, which become larger as they get nearer the Dead Sea.

Floodwaters leave behind sand and gravel. Jesus' story of the wise man who built his house on rock and the foolish man who built his house on sand (Matthew 7:24–27) is probably based on this phenomenon. According to the parable, a man built his house on the sand, in a flood zone. The rains fell, the floods came, and the house was destroyed. Another man built on the rock, out of the flood area, and the rains, though severe, had no impact on his house. Imagine someone building in the wadi pictured here. Jesus' audience must have chuckled at this story.

Overhead Transparency 26. Flood in the Wadi. When a flood does occur in the desert, it is amazing to behold. The sky is clear, the sun is shining, and suddenly a wall of water roars through the narrow canyon. Anyone unfortunate enough to be in the wadi is washed away—an all-too-frequent occurrence for shepherds and sheep in this region.

This photograph shows the floodwaters of a wadi cascading off a cliff near the Dead Sea in the Judea Wilderness.

Overhead Transparency 27. Quiet Waters in the Wilderness. After the rainy season and floods have passed, pools of water remain in the wadis, providing life to wilderness inhabitants. This pool in Wadi Zin in the Negev is a beautiful illustration of the still waters to which the shepherd guides his sheep. Sheep are undiscerning and will choose water that can be quite dangerous. That is why the shepherd must *lead* the sheep. It is the same with God and us human sheep. We are thirsty for fulfillment in our lives, and only God can guide us safely to that which will satisfy us. As the psalmist said: "He leads me beside quiet waters" (Psalm 23:2).

Step Two: "The Shepherd"

1. Lecture: Following the Shepherd

The theme of the shepherd is significant in the Bible. It appears more than 200 times, including more than 15 times in the New Testament. God chose the image of shepherd and sheep to explain His relationship with His people. He knew that the Israelites, as shepherds, would clearly understand the dynamic of this relationship. Sheep are helpless without a shepherd to lead them. They depend on the shepherd for their very survival. The shepherd guides them to pastures where they can eat and to pools where they can drink. The shepherd protects them from wild animals and brings them back to the flock when they get lost. Without a shepherd, sheep would die.

2. Guided Discussion: God Is Our Shepherd

Have your students look up the following passages and note how the image of the shepherd and his sheep is used to describe God and His people.

   a. Isaiah 40:10–11
   b. Genesis 49:24
   c. Psalm 95:6–7
   d. Psalm 78:52
   e. Psalm 100:3
   f. Luke 12:32
   g. Luke 15:4–7
   h. John 10:1–16

Ask your students to respond to the following questions:

1. Why do sheep need a shepherd?

2. What does it mean that God (or Jesus) is your Shepherd? Be specific.

3. What does it mean for you to be a member of a flock?

4. God used a common relationship—shepherd and sheep—as a picture of His relationship with His people. What relationships might reflect similar truth in today's culture?

OPTIONAL — Digging Deeper II: The Amalekites, King Saul, and Esther—God Keeps His Wilderness Promise

(27–35 minutes)

A. Lecture

Human beings, because of their selfish, sinful natures, can sometimes jeopardize God's plans for His people by pursuing their own desires rather than God's will. But God is patient and faithful. When we fail to do His bidding, He will often give us an opportunity to redeem ourselves by being obedient to Him. Israel's experience with the Amalekites in the wilderness is an example of God teaching His people this crucial lesson of obedience.

When the Israelites came out of Egypt, they were attacked by the Amalekites, a tribe of bedouins who lived in the Sinai Wilderness and the Negev. God, angered at the assault upon His people, instructed King Saul to totally destroy the Amalekites and all their possessions. But Saul was a self-centered, petty man who insisted on satisfying his own desires rather than doing what God had commanded. He spared Agag, the Amalekite king, and he kept the fattest sheep and cattle.

Because of Saul's persistent disobedience, his reign ended in failure. He was disgraced and abandoned by the people, his son Jonathan, David, Samuel, and even God.

Read the following passages aloud, and note the facts for your students:

- Exodus 17:8–16.

    1. Amalekites were desert nomads, descendants of Esau, who attacked the Israelites as they came out of Egypt.
    2. God promised to blot out the memory of Amalek from the earth, just as He will all those who assault His people.

- Deuteronomy 25:17–19.

    1. God considered the matter so important that He repeated His instructions and then added, "Don't forget!"

- 1 Samuel 15:1–3.

    1. God chose Saul for the task of punishing the Amalekites.

- 1 Samuel 15:9–11,27–29.

    1. Saul refused to be faithful to God in the task he was given. Like Achan (Joshua 7), he attempted to keep for himself what God had forbidden. Also, he left the Amalekite king, Agag, alive (1 Samuel 15:9), and evidently others as well.

King Saul's disobedience not only brought disgrace upon himself, but it also endangered the nation of Israel 400 years after his death.

- Esther 3:1–11.

  1. King Xerxes gave Haman permission to destroy the Jews. If this had happened, there would have been no Jesus, and we would all be condemned to hell.

  2. Haman was a descendant of Agag!

God, in His mercy, gave one of Saul's descendants, Esther, an opportunity to be faithful and thereby save the Israelites from the tragedy their ancestor Saul had created.

- Esther 2:5–7.

  1. God placed Esther (Hadassah) in a position to rescue His people and preserve His plan of salvation (Esther 4:12–14).

  2. Esther was a descendant of Kish, who was Saul's father (1 Samuel 9:1–2)!

B. Guided Discussion

Ask your students to address the following questions:

1. Failure to be faithful to God can reap terrible rewards, even hundreds of years later. Can you think of times God gave you an opportunity to act for Him and you failed? Can you imagine your failure creating a crisis for God's people long after your death? How?

2. God places us in the right place at the right time. Both Saul and Esther learned that. Saul refused to act as God wanted him to, but Esther was faithful. Think of an example of someone who was in the right place at the right time and was faithful to God. Tell the class.

3. Faithfulness to God can produce blessings generations after we are gone. Can you think of examples of people who were faithful in this way? (Examples: the disciples, the Pilgrims, missionaries who brought the gospel to your ancestors, grandparents who taught your parents about the Lord.) How might God reward your faithfulness in the lives of untold thousands of people years after you are in heaven?

OPTIONAL — Digging Deeper III: Understanding the Bible's Word Pictures (14–18 minutes)

A. Lecture: Word Pictures in the Bible

The early writers and readers of the Bible were Hebrew nomads living in the ancient Near East. They viewed their world in concrete, not abstract, terms. They described God and His relationship with them through word pictures and symbolic actions and not in formal definitions. For them, faith was a way of acting—a lifestyle. If we can learn to recognize and reflect on these word pictures, the Bible's message takes on an added richness.

B. Guided Discussion: The Use of Word Pictures

Ask students to describe their relationship with God. Note how many speak of God caring for them, saving them, loving them, watching over them. While these are wonderful ways of describing God, they would be foreign to the Israelite, for whom God is a shepherd or a rock.

Have your students (individually or in small groups) read the following passages and answer the questions.

1. What do the word pictures in the following scriptures reveal about God?

   a. John 6:35
   b. John 8:12
   c. Psalm 18:2
   d. Isaiah 25:1,4

2. What are the word pictures in the following scriptures? What do they reveal about you and your relationship with God?

   a. Isaiah 40:11
   b. Matthew 5:13–15
   c. Psalm 100:3
   d. John 3:3

3. What other word pictures in the Bible help us to understand God and our relationship with Him?

3. Guided Discussion: "Undershepherds"

The bedouins of today are semi-nomads who live in the wilderness areas of Israel and other Middle Eastern countries and retain much of the lifestyle of the ancient Israelites. The video *The Lord Is My Shepherd* noted that in today's bedouin culture, shepherds are often children, including girls. These children take care of the sheep while the adults handle the more difficult responsibilities of wilderness living. Young shepherds today pass the time playing flutelike instruments, hitting targets with sling-shots, and playing games. This was likely the case during biblical times as well.

Knowing this information about shepherds, how would your students interpret the following passages?

   a. 1 Samuel 16:1–13
   b. 1 Samuel 17:20,32–37,50

Often an adult shepherd oversees the children as they tend the sheep. This may explain the examples in the Bible in which shepherds are older. They were responsible for the combined flocks that children tended.

Ask a student to read aloud Exodus 2:11–17 (note the shepherdesses, some probably quite young, and the adult shepherds).

4. Personal Application

Some scholars believe that the practice of young shepherds tending sheep under the watchful eyes of the adult owners is the basis for the biblical picture of God, the chief Shepherd, appointing under-shepherds to care for His flock. Today we think of undershepherds as pastors, parents, teachers, or older brothers and sisters, to name a few.

Ask students to read aloud the following passages and answer the questions:

   a. John 21:15–17
   b. Numbers 27:15–17
   c. Ezekiel 34:1–24
   d. Acts 20:28
   e. Jeremiah 23:1–4
   f. 1 Peter 5:2–4

1. How does God give you responsibility to care for part of His flock today? (Examples: taking care of younger brothers and sisters, teaching Sunday school, coaching a Little League team.) How are you under the leadership of His undershepherds?

2. Consider the image of young shepherds caring for the flock of an older owner. What does that word picture teach about your attitude toward those for whom you are responsible?

3. What should your attitude be toward those who are responsible for leading you?

4. The cultural practice of leading sheep means the sheep must be close enough to see and hear the shepherd. It also means that the children who work for the adult shepherd represent his voice and his leading of the sheep. How do these practices relate to our need to be in contact with our Shepherd? How do they relate to the responsibility we have as undershepherds to Jesus?

5. Based on Jeremiah 23:1–4, what type of shepherd are you, and what is your responsibility to the flock to which you belong?

6. How will you be a more faithful undershepherd on behalf of the great Shepherd? Write down an example, and if you desire, relate it to the class. How might you be a more faithful member of the flock? Write a brief statement, and discuss your answer with the class.

* * * * * * * * * *

5. Guided Discussion: Being Led by the Shepherd

In our Western world, shepherds and their dogs drive sheep ahead of them. By contrast, shepherds in the Middle East lead their sheep. Travelers to Israel are often amazed to see large flocks of sheep following young bedouin shepherds who are some distance in front of them and who rarely look back to see if the flocks are following.

Have your students read the following passages and answer the questions:

a. Psalm 77:20
b. Psalm 78:52
c. Exodus 13:21–22
d. Isaiah 40:11
e. Isaiah 49:9b–10
f. John 10:2–5,14–18

1. What picture best describes God's leading Israel from Egypt to the Promised Land?

2. What physical phenomenon did Israel follow? NOTE: Some scholars argue that the Hebrew tendency to apply concrete images to supernatural occurrences explains the early biblical writers' portrayal of the cloud of fire and smoke as God's feet. In Exodus 13:21–22, the Hebrew word translated "went" ahead of them could be "walked" ahead of them. Note also that in Exodus 33:10, the cloud *stood* at the entrance to the tabernacle.

3. In what ways does God the Shepherd lead His sheep today? How is His voice heard?

4. What happens if a sheep does not follow the shepherd? How might this apply to the Christian life?

5. A rabbi said, "Whatever you follow in life is the voice of your shepherd. If you follow something other than God, you cannot call Him your shepherd." Think of an example of someone who believes God is his Shepherd but who follows another voice (e.g., a teenager who has committed her life to Christ but who watches immoral movies, a man who belongs to a church but who is unethical in his business practices). Relate the example to the class.

6. Guided Discussion: Green Pastures

The regions in Israel where shepherds live have two seasons: the rainy season from November through March, when even the desert becomes green, and the dry season from April through October, when the landscape is completely brown. One would think that pasture would be plentiful in the rainy season, but shepherds struggle to find adequate pasture year round. Because crop farmers use all the arable land, shepherds are restricted to marginal areas of the wilderness for their grazing animals.

Pastures of the Middle East are quite different from what many Westerners envision. The lush grasslands we find in North America don't exist in Israel. Sheep get enough nourishment for the moment, but no more. Day to day, the sheep must depend on their shepherd to lead them to the food and water they need to survive.

Have your students (individually or in small groups) reflect on the following questions:

a. Describe your image of green pastures, and apply that picture to the Christian life. (Students will probably describe pastures with an abundance of grass.) Is this what living with God is like? Do we really have what we need for the future?

b. Recall a situation that you didn't think you could handle. How did God provide? Did you receive everything you needed for the whole experience or just enough for the moment at hand? How is this like the green pastures of the shepherd?

c. Why don't sheep have to worry? Why is worry wrong for the sheep of God's flock? (Note Matthew 6:25–34.)

d. Read Exodus 16:4–5,17–30. How was the gift of manna like green pastures? How did each involve faith in God?

e. Why is it so critical for sheep to stay in contact with the shepherd? How does that relate to you as you follow Jesus?

Ask your students to recall a time when they learned that God provides only for the moment. Have them take a few minutes to speak to God and ask for the faith to trust Him for every second of their lives and to give thanks for the "green pastures" of past experiences.

OPTIONAL — Digging Deeper IV: Floods in the Desert (12–17 minutes)

(HINT: *If you have the optional full-color overhead-transparency packet, it might be helpful at this point for the class to view or re-view the overhead transparencies in* **Digging Deeper I** *of this lesson.*)

A. Lecture

Although the wilderness of Israel gets little rainfall, the central mountains get a great deal of moisture during the winter months. The thin topsoil of the mountains is not able to absorb the large quantities of water, which run into the valleys to the Mediterranean in the west and the wilderness to the east and south. In the wilderness, the dry valleys (called wadis) quickly fill with raging streams that sweep away anything in their paths as they descend to the Dead Sea. These floods pose great danger to shepherds and their sheep. Even today it is not uncommon for people and animals to drown in wadis, as flash floods can occur even when the sky is clear, because the rains fall some distance away.

The raging waters leave behind refreshing pools, and it is the task of the shepherd to determine if these are safe for his flock to drink and lie beside—if they are the "quiet waters" referred to by the psalmist (Psalm 23:2). The term still carries a double meaning, referring both to calm water and to a safe location.

B. Guided Discussion

Ask your students to read the following passages and then answer the questions:

- Psalm 69:1–3a
- Psalm 124:1–5
- Isaiah 32:2
- Psalm 126:1–4

Dry wilderness valleys would periodically fill with raging water from flash floods. What does this image add to the passages you just read? Why must we follow the Shepherd to water?

NOTE: One difference between the wadis of the Judea Wilderness and those of the Negev is that the latter collect rainfall from a much wider area, transforming thousands of tiny streams into a roaring torrent. Thus, in Psalm 126:1–4, the writer asked for a blessing that begins as a small stream and becomes a large river.

7. Guided Discussion: The Lost Sheep

The numerous trails crisscrossing hills are a striking feature of Israel's wilderness. Grazing flocks formed these tracks over thousands of years. Sometimes the trails lead to the edge of a cliff and the only escape is to retreat. Because there are so many of them, the trails are difficult to use as hiking paths. They rarely go directly to any destination and often cross other trails as they wander along steep hillsides. In this setting, the idea of a lost sheep, the basis of so many Bible passages, is easy to understand.

Ask your students to read the following scriptures and explain their meanings based on the confusing paths of the wilderness.

a. Matthew 18:12–14
b. Jeremiah 50:6
c. Proverbs 2:12–15
d. Proverbs 3:5–6
e. Psalm 23:3 (NOTE: The Hebrew word for *righteousness* can also mean "straight.")

1. Think of examples where life's "paths" were confusing—that is, where the choices of direction or action were unclear or where the right choice was difficult to recognize. Discuss your examples with the class.

2. Think of an example where the choice of the wrong path had (or could have had) serious consequences. If you desire, relate your example to the class.

3. Read Proverbs 3:5–6 and Psalm 23:3 again. What is the promise the Shepherd gives concerning the confusion of paths in life? How does that apply to your walk in life right now?

4. Read Psalm 23:4. The Hebrew text says, ". . . the valley of the deepest [or darkest] shadow." Given the confusing nature of the paths on steep wilderness hillsides, especially in Judea, the presence of the shepherd is particularly important in times of danger. Note that this is the one place in Psalm 23 where the Shepherd is not in front of you but beside you. Reflect on an experience of the "darkest" shadow . . . maybe even the shadow of death. How was God beside you at that moment? Discuss your answer with the class.

Close this lesson with a few moments of prayer to the Shepherd, asking His day-by-day provision for each member of His flock.

Conclusion

This lesson is based on (1) the lifestyle of the Middle Eastern shepherd and (2) the nature of the wilderness where he pastures his sheep. The shepherd's knowledge of the wilderness and the dangers sheep will encounter if they wander away highlight the importance of our always staying close to and following God. As sheep, we are helpless without our Shepherd to guide and protect us. He leads us to green pastures and still waters where we can rest. He stands between us and those who seek to kill and devour us. But it is up to us to stay close enough to Him that we are always able to see and hear Him.

Ask your students to take five minutes to write their responses to the following:

a. Describe an occasion when God led you through a time of trouble.

b. When have you been a shepherd to someone else for God?

As you end this lesson, pray that your students will continue to keep their eyes on their Shepherd and listen to His voice.

NOT ON BREAD ALONE

Israel is mostly rugged desert. The variety of Hebrew words for *desert* or *wilderness* indicates the significant role the landscape played in biblical history and imagery. For the Hebrews, the desert was far more formative than the sea, probably because of their desert roots (which caused them to fear the ocean) and because there were few seaports along the Mediterranean coast.

Most of the year, the desert is an uncultivated area receiving just enough rainfall during the winter months to sustain the nomadic shepherds who live there. The deserts of the Bible are more rock than sand and are often quite mountainous. The two most significant wilderness areas in Israel are the Judea Wilderness in the east and the Negev in the south.

THE JUDEA WILDERNESS

The Judea Mountains form the middle section of the central mountain range of Israel. On the eastern side of this ridge, descending into the Great Rift Valley more than 1,300 feet below sea level, is the solitary, rocky wasteland of Judah. Because of the change in altitude, little rain falls here. The land is split by deep wadis formed by centuries of rain runoff in the mountains, and even shepherds find it difficult to live here. This wilderness borders the fertile mountain ridge for more than 50 miles, so the line between farmland and wilderness is a clear one. Throughout biblical times, shepherds lived on the fringes of the desert, and farmers worked the soil of the mountains. Villages like Bethlehem were able to sustain both shepherds (David) and farmers (Boaz and Ruth).

THE NEGEV

The Negev lies south of the Hebron Mountains, which form the southern section of Israel's central mountain range. This arid land (*Negev* means "dry") has few natural water sources and receives less than eight inches of rainfall in the north and less than half that amount in the south. Except for a few settlements that employ advanced methods to catch rain runoff, the Negev is nonarable, hospitable only to nomads.

The northern region of the Negev, from the Hebron Mountains to the Zin Wilderness, is good sheep country. Its rolling hills surround large, broad valleys—such as the Valley of Beersheba, where Abraham settled.

The central region of the Negev is rugged, with deep canyons in the Zin Wilderness. The climate and terrain are inhospitable, even to nomads, for most of the year. At least one scholar has suggested that the "valley of the shadow of death" (Psalm 23) may refer to the canyons of the central Negev.

The southern portion of the Negev is called the Wilderness of Paran in the Bible and is the most barren area of all.

WANDERING IN THE WILDERNESS

It was in the Negev and the Sinai Wilderness to the south and west that the children of Israel wandered after God miraculously delivered them from Egypt. They received the Torah on Mount Sinai and built the tabernacle at the base of the mountain. When they reached the northern edge of the Negev, the Israelites sent spies into Canaan to discover the nature of their new home. Upon hearing the spies' reports of giants and huge fortified cities, the Israelites grew afraid and refused to enter the Promised Land. Because they were disobedient and lacked faith, God commanded His people to remain in the wilderness, where they wandered for 40 years, a year for each day the spies had been gone. The Bible records the place as "the vast and dreadful desert" (Deuteronomy 8:15).

In the wilderness, God taught His people faith and trust, preparing them to live obediently in the Promised Land *so that the world might know that He was God.* He sent them water from rock, manna from heaven, and quail from the sea. Their feet did not swell (a remarkable blessing to anyone who has hiked in the Negev), and their clothes did not wear out (Deuteronomy 8:4).

In the wilderness, God disciplined His people for their lack of faith, their disobedience, and their complaining. Moses recorded that God humbled them so they would learn to depend on Him for everything, because "man does not live on bread alone but on every word that comes from the mouth of the LORD" (Deuteronomy 8:3–5).

LESSONS OF THE WILDERNESS

The Jewish people's 40-year journey in the wilderness made a significant impact on them. The psalmist reminded the Hebrews of God's faithful love in the wilderness (Psalms 105:38–45 and 107:4–9) and warned them against repeating their earlier sins (Psalms 81:11–16 and 78:14–40). The prophets recalled to the people's minds the lessons learned there (Jeremiah 2:6 and 7:22–25; Micah 6:3–5), and the writers of the New Testament compared the experience to the lives of believers (Hebrews 3:16–19; 1 Corinthians 10:1–13). In Judea, when Jesus, as the new "Adam," faced the tempter on our behalf, He used the lessons of the wilderness to defeat him: "Man does not live on bread alone" (Matthew 4:4; see also Deuteronomy 8:3) and "Do not put the LORD your God to the test" (Matthew 4:7; see also Deuteronomy 6:16).

WILDERNESS AS REFUGE

Because the wilderness was so close to settled areas, it became a refuge for those who sought solitude or safety from authorities. Here David hid from Saul's anger (1 Samuel 26), John the Baptist isolated himself from the religious practices of the day (Matthew 3), and Jesus faced the devil (Matthew 4). Here the Essenes labored over their scrolls and early Christians built monasteries, some of which still function today.

The wilderness was also associated with the coming of the Messiah. Isaiah 40:3–4 says, "In the desert prepare the way for the LORD; make straight in the wilderness a highway for our God. Every valley shall be raised up, every mountain and hill made low." When Jesus entered Jerusalem on Palm Sunday, He came from the wilderness, which might have added to the crowd's fervor.

CONCLUSION

The wilderness image is a rich one in the Bible. It refers to our lives here on earth as we prepare for our "promised land" in heaven. It portrays those difficult times in our lives when we learn to trust the faithful provision of our God. The wilderness also offers a picture of God's disciplining us for our sinful lives. And it reminds us of the Messiah's eventual return.

In the wilderness, we learn that we cannot live on bread alone.

GOD WITH US

For the Teacher

The people of the Old Testament worshiped God differently from the way we do. For example, they sacrificed animals daily, and they were commanded to do this only in Jerusalem. This lesson explores the ceremonies and structures the Israelites used to establish and develop their relationship with God. Our story is set at Arad, a city dating to the time of Hezekiah. In this lesson, your students will learn to identify with biblical people, events, and settings as they come to understand the nature of the temple and the covenant God established with His people through Moses, David, and Solomon. Emphasize throughout that we can learn about God and how to worship Him by exploring the similarities between the worship practices of the Canaanite culture and those of the Israelites and by noting the way God communicated His unique message to His people. The most amazing discovery your students may make is that the Israelites' religious practices pointed to Jesus more than a thousand years before He was born and that heaven itself was the pattern for their temple and its worship services.

As you begin this lesson, encourage your students to see themselves as part of a line of people that begins in the Bible and continues until Jesus returns. People like Abraham, David, and Solomon, though from a different culture than our own, experienced the same God and His love that we do today. As your students explore the remains of the long-forgotten city of Arad, they will find clear parallels between the lives of its people and their own lives. As often as possible, draw connections between the archaeological remains and the modern-day practices and settings familiar to your students. Your enthusiasm for understanding God's saving work through the people of the Bible can become the means by which your students discover that God is with us today just as He was with the Israelites centuries ago.

Your Objectives for This Lesson

At the completion of this section, you will want your students:

To Know/Understand

1. The significance of the city of Arad in the Old Testament, its role in Israel's history, and the archaeological discoveries made there.

2. The impact of the religious reforms begun by King Hezekiah on the worship experience of the Israelites and the city of Arad.

3. The relationship between the temple at Arad and Solomon's temple at Jerusalem.

4. The function of each element of the temple at Arad and how it illustrates the nature of the worship of God.

5. The relationship between God's covenant with Abraham and Jesus' death on the cross, and the common symbolism of blood.

6. The nature of a covenant and the ceremony and items used to establish it.

7. The reality of the presence of God in believers today who have become "God's temple" (1 Corinthians 3:16).

To Do

1. Conduct an inventory of their lives to determine that God alone is the object of their worship.

2. Commit to examining their worship experiences so that they reflect the characteristics of true worship.

3. Thank God for His willingness to pay with His own blood for their covenant breaking.

4. Read the Ten Commandments to hear an affirmation of God's statement "I love you."

5. Develop a plan to represent the presence of God regularly to at least one person.

6. Lay at Jesus' feet all unresolved sin and guilt that is preventing them from being God's instruments.

7. Follow the biblical practice and establish a regular prayer time as an expression of their relationships with God.

How to Plan for This Lesson

Because of the volume of material in this lesson, you may need to divide it into several class sessions. To help you determine how to do that, the lesson has been broken into segments that can each be covered in approximately one hour. The end of each of these segments is marked by a row of asterisks.

If, however, you need to cover the entire lesson in one 60-minute session, you should include the following elements in your lesson plan:

- Step One—sections 1–5
- Step Two—sections 3(a) and 5

How to Prepare for This Lesson

Materials Needed

Student copies of the maps:	"The Divided Kingdom" "Topography of Israel" "Israel"
Overhead transparencies:	"The Divided Kingdom" "Topography of Israel" "Chronology of Bible Times" "The First Temple at Jerusalem" "The Temple at Arad" "Israel"
Student copies of the handouts:	"A Covenant Guarantee" "The Ark of God"

Video: **God with Us**

Overhead projector, screen, VCR

1. Make copies of the "Divided Kingdom," "Topography of Israel," and "Israel" maps for your students.

2. Prepare the overhead transparencies "The Divided Kingdom," "Topography of Israel," "Chronology of Bible Times," "The First Temple at Jerusalem," "The Temple at Arad," and "Israel."

3. Make copies of the handouts "A Covenant Guarantee" and "The Ark of God" for your students. (If possible, students should receive and read these handouts before the lesson.)

4. Determine which optional **Digging Deeper** sections, if any, you want to use in your class session(s). NOTE: You can use these sections in any order you wish (e.g., you might want to use **Digging Deeper III**, but not **Digging Deeper I** or **Digging Deeper II**).

5. Review the geography of the lands of the Bible from the "Introduction" and the map study sections in Lessons 6 and 8. Review the nature of Baal worship in Lesson 6.

6. Prepare your classroom ahead of time, setting up and testing an overhead projector and screen and a VCR. If you plan to hand out biblical references for students to look up and read aloud, prepare 3x5 cards (one reference per card) to distribute before class.

Lesson Plan

Step One: "The City of Arad"

1. Introductory Comments: The Temple at Arad

In this lesson, we are going to study one of the most unique archaeological discoveries of recent times: the Israelite temple at the city of Arad. Solomon's temple at Jerusalem was destroyed by the Babylonians in 586 B.C., leaving no remains for scholars to study. Since the Arad temple dates to the time of Solomon's temple and follows the same basic pattern, archaeologists excavated it to gain insight into the structure of the temple at Jerusalem. The people of the small community of Arad worshiped the same God who was honored in Jerusalem and the same God we glorify today. The archaeological remains of these God-fearing people provide significant insight into ancient religious practices. And as we will see, God established principles of worship that anticipated the life and ministry of Jesus and that provide the basis for our worship today.

HINT: *At this point, ask the students to imagine people almost 3,000 years ago worshiping the same God we do today. Ask how they feel about the fact that we are part of a line of people following Yahweh and used by Him that begins with Adam and Eve and will not end until Jesus' second coming. Responses should be brief but substantive enough to stimulate students to begin thinking about the importance of understanding these ancient people as our spiritual ancestors.*

2. Map Study: The City of Arad

HINT: *As your students learn the location of Arad in the Negev, help them recognize that the Israelites had roots in this region through Abraham and Moses.*

Using the overhead transparency "The Divided Kingdom," ask your students to find the following locations on their maps.

   Israel (northern tribes)
   Samaria
   Jerusalem

Lachish
Judah (southern tribes; note border with northern tribes)
the Negev
Arad

Using the overhead transparency "Topography of Israel," ask your students to find the following locations on their maps.

the Dead Sea   the Negev
Beersheba   the coastal plain
Arad   the Judea Mountains
the Hebron Mountains

3. Review the Overhead Transparency "Chronology of Bible Times"

Using the overhead transparency "Chronology of Bible Times," highlight the following dates for your students:

1900 B.C.	Abraham goes to Canaan
1000 B.C.	David, Solomon (temple built)
900 B.C.	Kingdom divides
700 B.C.	Hezekiah, Assyria destroys Samaria (north), Sennacherib attacks Judah (south)
586 B.C.	Judah falls to Babylonians (temple destroyed)
500 B.C.	Nehemiah, Ezra (temple rebuilt)
37–4 B.C.	Herod (second temple rebuilt)
A.D. 70	Second temple destroyed

4. Lecture: The Center of Israelite Life—The Temple

Point out the following facts to your students:

- Through Abraham, God established a relationship with the Israelites that was unique among nations.

- Moses built the tabernacle and established the worship practices God gave him on Mount Sinai.

- David collected the building materials and selected a location, and his son Solomon built the temple.

- Throughout Israel's history, even during times of pagan worship, the temple remained the center of religious life. It was during Hezekiah's reign that laws were passed establishing Jerusalem as the official place of worship and outlawing other worship locations.

5. View the Video *God with Us* (31 minutes)

6. Guided Discussion: Arad Was in the Negev

Ask students to read aloud the following passages:

- Genesis 12:1–9

- Genesis 13:1–2

- Genesis 20:1

Note that Abraham lived at times in the Negev, the region where the city of Arad is located.

- Numbers 21:1–3a
- Joshua 12:14 (a list of kings conquered by Joshua)

Note that the Israelites fought against Arad and eventually settled it.

7. Guided Discussion: The People of Arad Worshiped Yahweh

a. *Lecture: Archaeological Remains*

Archaeologists believe the inhabitants of Arad worshiped Yahweh and not pagan idols. At the site, archaeologists discovered the following items:

- Ostraca (potsherds with writing on them) inscribed with the names of priests mentioned in the Bible. Other names on the ostraca were Yahwistic (containing part of God's name), like "Eshiyahu." **HINT:** *It might be helpful to review the handout "My God Is Yahweh" in Lesson 7 and the discussion of that material within the lesson.*
- Bowls inscribed "Sons of Bezalel" (see Exodus 31:1–11).
- An offering bowl inscribed "Sacred for the Priests."
- A temple similar in design and size to the tabernacle and the temple at Jerusalem.

Clearly, the inhabitants of Arad, living almost 3,000 years ago, were God-fearing people. They are our spiritual brothers and sisters whom we will likely meet in heaven someday.

b. *Personal Application*

Ask a student to read aloud Hebrews 12:1. Then have the class respond to the following questions:

1. How might the people of Arad be part of the "cloud of witnesses"?
2. How do they strengthen your faith?
3. How will we be remembered by the generations after us? Do the physical things we leave behind testify to our faith in God? How?
4. What might we do to leave a God-honoring legacy behind?

Pray that each member of the class would be as strong and unswerving in faith as the inhabitants of Arad and that he or she would leave behind a faith record that others can emulate.

* * * * * * * * * *

Step Two: "The Temple at Arad"

1. Lecture: The Layout of the Temples at Jerusalem and Arad

To help your students understand the basic layout of the temples at Jerusalem and Arad, prepare Overhead Transparencies 11 ("The First Temple at Jerusalem") and 12 ("The Temple at Arad"), and point out the following elements. NOTE: You don't need to go into detail here, because a more in-depth discussion of the different elements of the temples will be given in Guided Discussion 3 below.

- a. The Worship Court
    1. The Altar of Sacrifice
    2. The Bronze Sea (basin)

b. The Holy Place

    1. The Table of Showbread

    2. The Lampstand

    3. The Altars of Incense (The temple at Jerusalem had only one.)

c. The Holy of Holies

    1. The Ark with the Tablets of the Covenant, or the Ten Commandments

2. Guided Discussion: The Temple at Arad

a. *Lecture*

The people of Israel and Judah were relentlessly drawn into the worship of Canaanite gods, particularly Baal. (**HINT:** *It might be helpful to consult Lessons 6 and 7 and the handout "The Fertility Cults of Canaan" in Lesson 6 for a review of the material on the worship of this fertility god.*) Godly kings like Hezekiah and Josiah struggled to keep the people faithful to Yahweh and His values. To prevent the Israelites from worshiping pagan gods, these kings ordered the destruction of all high places (to Yahweh as well as Baal). One of these worship locations was the city of Arad. Most scholars believe the temple at Arad, used in the worship of Israel's God, was buried approximately 715 B.C. at Hezekiah's command. Because it was covered up, it wasn't destroyed when invading armies captured the city. It is still well preserved today.

b. *Personal Application*

Ask the class to respond to these questions:

1. Can you think of modern-day "Hezekiahs"—people or organizations (e.g., Promise Keepers)?

2. Are your responses to our society's cultural decline different from Hezekiah's because he was a king and you are not? Specifically, what are your responses, and how do they differ from Hezekiah's, if they do?

Point to Ponder: One of the long-term benefits of Hezekiah's reforms is the preserved temple at Arad. Though the benefit may be minor when compared with the blessings the Israelites enjoyed at the time of the reforms, the lessons to be learned from the archaeology of Arad are quite significant for our lives today. God is *still* blessing Hezekiah's faithfulness.

OPTIONAL — Digging Deeper I: The Faithfulness of Kings Hezekiah and Josiah *(25–27 minutes)*

Guided Discussion

The religious revival wrought by Hezekiah was significant and brought God's immediate blessing to Judah. The reforms of Josiah, approximately 60 years later, were even more striking. Have students (individually or in small groups) look up and summarize the following passages:

a. The kings after Hezekiah:

- 2 Chronicles 33:1–9. How could Manasseh, the son of the faithful Hezekiah, be so unfaithful?

- 2 Chronicles 33:10–13 (especially verse 13). Note God's discipline and Manasseh's response.

- 2 Chronicles 33:21–24. Was Manasseh's repentance too late to influence his son Amon? Apply this idea to the role of young parents. Why is it important to make God and His values central to our families from the start?

b. The faithful Josiah:

- 2 Chronicles 34:1–3a. How old was Josiah when he was "converted"?

- 2 Chronicles 34:3b. How old was Josiah when he began to put his faith into practice? Typically, how old are the members of your church community when they are encouraged to put their faith into practice?

- 2 Chronicles 34:3b–7. What specific actions did Josiah take to eliminate the pagan practices and attitudes of his kingdom? How would you apply this concept today? Does it have both personal and community applications? What are they?

- 2 Chronicles 34:14–21,29–32. What did Josiah do to restore the faith of his people? What could you do today to have a similar influence on your family? On your friends? On your community? Can you identify a modern-day "Josiah"—either a person, an organization, or a movement? How can you become a Josiah?

c. Ask your students to read Exodus 12:14–15. Notice that the Israelites were to remove all yeast from their houses *before* Passover. In Jewish tradition, this yeast represented physical impurity and uncleanness that must be removed from homes before the people could celebrate the great feast of deliverance. In later tradition, the yeast represented the need to remove sin from the people's lives (like leaven from their homes) before they could celebrate Passover. Many Christian communities continue this practice (without even knowing its connection to Passover) by having a time of self-preparation before the Lord's Supper. Ask your students to read the following passages and respond to the questions:

- 2 Chronicles 34:33—The "yeast" of idolatry was removed.

- 2 Chronicles 35:1,6—The Passover was held.

- 2 Chronicles 35:16–19—No greater Passover had ever been held, in part because of the thorough way Josiah had removed the "yeast" of paganism from the land.

- 1 Corinthians 11:27–29—The Lord's Supper demands similar removal of "yeast." (Note 1 Corinthians 5:6–8.)

   1. How will you apply this concept of the removal of yeast in your life? If you desire, briefly relate your answer to the class.

   2. How could the Christian community help remove the yeast in our culture?

d. Ask your students to read 2 Chronicles 35:20–25. Josiah was killed on the plain of Megiddo, known to history as the Valley of Armageddon. The struggle between good and evil, between God's followers and those who follow the evil one, continues today.

   1. Why did Jeremiah compose laments about Josiah's death?

   2. Turn the page of your Bible. How soon after the loss of this great reformer king did the end of Judah come? Count up the years of reign for each of the remaining kings. Why is obedience to God critical?

Ask your students to spend a few moments in prayer, specifically asking God to protect strong Christian leaders and give them the courage to act obediently before it's too late.

3. Guided Discussion: A Comparison of the Temples at Jerusalem and Arad

This guided discussion is divided into several parts, each corresponding to the structure of the temples at Jerusalem and Arad. Each section begins with a review of the overhead transparencies "The First Temple at Jerusalem" and "The Temple at Arad" and then examines an element of the temples.

a. *The Courts of the Temple*

Both the Arad and the Jerusalem temples had three courts: the worship court, the holy place, and the Holy of Holies. The temple at Arad was built in a style similar to the average Israelite house (which was probably influenced by Egyptian architecture), and the temple at Jerusalem followed the Phoenician-Syrian temple design.

1. The *worship court* was a large outer court where the people stood to worship. It contained the altar of sacrifice and the laver or basin (the Bronze Sea).

2. The *holy place*, or priests' court, was a rectangular room between the worship court and the Holy of Holies. It contained the table of showbread, the golden lampstand, and the altars of incense. (The temple at Jerusalem had only one altar.)

    a. At Arad, the holy place was positioned lengthwise, with its longest walls opening to the worship court on one side and the Holy of Holies on the other side. (See diagram below.) This style brought the people in the worship court closer to the priest in his room and to God in the Holy of Holies. It was called the broad room. At Jerusalem, the holy place was positioned in the opposite way. The worship court and the Holy of Holies were at each end of the rectangle, with the length of the holy place between. (See diagram below.) This style moved the people farther away from the priest in his room and from God in the Holy of Holies. It was called the long room.

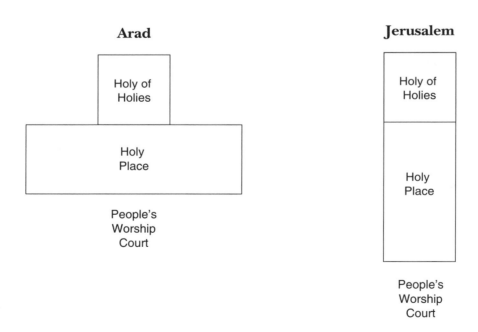

    b. Ask your students to read 2 Chronicles 2:3–7,11–14 and then answer the questions. Tyre is part of Phoenicia. Christians often assume that God chose a unique style for His temple. In fact, He selected a well-known design that was much older than His temple.

        • Why would God have chosen an existing style?

- What does this say about Christians using cultural means to spread God's message (i.e., technologies and practices known to the culture)? How can we avoid the sinful aspects of the culture at large?

- Some scholars have noted that the Phoenician-Syrian, long-room style that Solomon chose for the temple at Jerusalem accentuated the priest by moving the people in the outer court away from the Holy of Holies. Why would God have wanted a style that accentuated the priest? (Could it be because Jesus was to fulfill the role of our high priest? By turning the room in this way, the importance of the priest is accentuated, making anticipation for the High Priest Jesus greater. With this temple design, God was saying, "I want the priest to be very important, because someday the ultimate fulfillment of the priest is going to be Jesus Christ.") NOTE: After the class has responded to this question, ask a student to read aloud Hebrews 8:3–6 and 9:11.

3. The *Holy of Holies* contained the ark of the covenant with the tablets of the covenant, or the Ten Commandments.

* * * * * * * * * *

b. *Other Elements of the Temples at Jerusalem and Arad*

1. The *altar of sacrifice* was in the outer worship court. Have your students read the following passages, which describe God's instructions for building the altar of the tabernacle. Then ask them to answer the questions:

- Exodus 20:25—Arad's altar is made of uncut stones.

- Exodus 27:1—Arad's altar is the same size.

    a. What did the altar symbolize? (See Leviticus 17:6,11.)

      1. Read Hebrews 9:22. What does this altar ultimately represent? What does it mean to you that God's people, Israel, sacrificed here more than 700 years before Jesus?

      2. What do you think it was like to have hundreds of animals killed every day, their blood sprinkled on altars, their carcasses cut up, and some parts burned? The stench of blood, gore, and burning flesh must have been suffocating. How would this have indicated to the Israelites the awful penalty of sin?

    b. At what times were the daily sacrifices made? (See Numbers 28:3–8.) Though there is debate as to exactly what hours the early Israelites offered these sacrifices, by the time of Jesus, the morning offering was made at approximately 9:00 and the afternoon sacrifice was made at approximately 3:00. It appears that these times were established early in the history of the temple service. After the rebuilding of the Jerusalem temple (by Zerubbabel—see Ezra 3, and note especially Ezra 3:3, 9:5, and Acts 3:1), daily prayers were said at these times as well. So we can say that for centuries, God's people knew that an offering was being made for their sins every day at 9:00 and 3:00.

      Have your students read 1 Kings 18:36, 2 Kings 16:15, and Acts 10:30. Then turn together to Matthew 27:46–50, and ask the class to answer the following questions:

      1. What time did Jesus die?

      2. What was happening at the temple at that time?

      3. What had happened at that time every day for centuries?

      4. What was God saying?

Take a few minutes to reflect on God's careful plan for the death of Jesus and its meaning in the context of Jewish tradition. If students wish, let them relate their reactions to the class. Then spend a few minutes in prayer, thanking God for the powerful context of Jesus' death and for His having replaced all those sacrifices.

HINT: *If you have the optional full-color overhead-transparency packet, prepare Overhead Transparencies 30 ("The Outer Court of the Temple at Arad"), 31 ("The Holy Place of the Temple at Arad"), and 32 ("The Holy of Holies of the Temple at Arad") for the next two sections.*

2. The *Bronze Sea* was a metal basin that stood in the outer worship court. The priest used the water in the basin for ceremonial cleansing, which symbolized (a) the removal of ceremonial uncleanness before the sacrifice was offered and (b) the forgiveness resulting from the sacrifice itself. For a more in-depth study of this object, see **Digging Deeper III**, Overhead Transparency 30, in this lesson.

3. The *table of showbread*, or table of "the bread of the Presence," was in the holy place, or priests' court. The bread offered by the priest symbolized a thanksgiving gift to God, as well as a request for God's provision of food. For a more in-depth study, see **Digging Deeper III**, Overhead Transparency 31.

4. The *golden lampstand* was located in the holy place in front of the veil covering the Holy of Holies. Although scholars debate the lampstand's actual configuration, it did have seven lamps and was made of pure gold. God showed Moses the pattern when Moses met with Him on Mount Sinai (Numbers 8:4). The lampstand was to provide continual light before the Lord. The seven lamps probably symbolized completeness, and the light represented the presence of God in the tabernacle and later in the temple. The people provided oil to keep the lamps burning from evening until morning because, according to Jewish tradition, they were a reflection of God's glory (Exodus 27:2–21). Solomon apparently made 10 of these lampstands for the first temple at Jerusalem (2 Chronicles 4:7).

5. The *altars of incense* were in the holy place, on either side of the entrance to the Holy of Holies. The Jerusalem temple had only one altar. Have a student read aloud Exodus 30:1–9. This altar represented the prayers of God's people going up to Him. Ask the class to read the following passages and answer the questions:

   - Psalm 141:2
   - Revelation 5:8
   - Revelation 8:3–4
   - Luke 1:8–17 (This was probably the first time Zechariah did this. There were hundreds of priests in his order who served two weeks per year, and no one could repeat the offering of incense until the others had taken their turns.)

     1. What can you learn from the ceremonies that came before the incense (prayer) offering? (What had to be passed first?)
     2. Why was the altar directly in front of the Holy of Holies?
     3. What takes the place of the incense offering in your life?

6. The *ark of the covenant* and the tablets of the *Ten Commandments* were located in the Holy of Holies. **Digging Deeper III**, Overhead Transparency 32, goes into more detail about the standing stones found here. Have your students read the handout "A Covenant Guarantee" before beginning this section.

   In the ancient Near East, there was a special covenant form in which a greater party, often a king, established a relationship with a lesser party, often a vassal. The superior party decided the responsibilities of each party, and the lesser party accepted or rejected the relationship. God deals with His people in this kind of covenant.

For each of the following passages, ask your students to note (1) what in the context makes God the superior party with the right to make a covenant, (2) God's promises within the relationship, and (3) the person through whom God made the covenant.

- Genesis 9:8–17
- Genesis 15:18 and 17:2
- Exodus 19:3–6 and 24:3–8
- 2 Samuel 7:12–16 (compare 23:5)
- Luke 22:19–20

Have your students read Hebrews 13:19–20 and answer the question: What does it mean to you that God has made a covenant with you through Jesus?

* * * * * * * * *

OPTIONAL — Digging Deeper II: The Bronze Sea (15–17 minutes)

Guided Discussion

Point out to your students the many striking parallels between God's dwelling place in heaven and His earthly home, the temple.

HEAVEN	TEMPLE
God's dwelling place (Matthew 6:9)	God's dwelling place (2 Chronicles 6:21)
God surrounded by cherubim (Revelation 4:6b–8 [Ezekiel 1:6,10])	God surrounded by figures of cherubim (2 Chronicles 3:10–13)
God surrounded by His heavenly hosts (Revelation 5:11)	God surrounded by His earthly hosts (Numbers 2)
God is seated on a throne (Revelation 4:2–5)	Ark is God's throne (Psalm 99:1)
Altar representing the blood of the saints (Revelation 6:9)	Blood sprinkled on the altar (Leviticus 1:10–11)
Incense as the prayers of the saints (Revelation 5:8)	Altar of incense where the priest met with God (Exodus 30:1,6)
Sea of crystal (Revelation 4:6)	Sea of bronze (1 Kings 7:23)

People often view the crystal sea as a large ocean, but it actually indicates a basin or laver of crystal. Does this change your perception of the crystal sea?

OPTIONAL — Digging Deeper III: The Temple at Arad—Visual Insights

(20–25 minutes)

(This section requires the use of the optional full-color overhead-transparency packet. If you need information on ordering it, see inside front cover.)

The temple at Arad is a remarkable archaeological find. It dates to the time of Solomon's temple at Jerusalem, and because Solomon's temple is no longer standing, the Arad temple provides insight into its construction and function.

The following overhead transparencies show different elements of the temple at Arad.

Overhead Transparency 28. Tel Arad. The fortress city of Arad was located at the edge of the Negev wilderness and guarded the back door to Jerusalem. The Canaanite city that stood here apparently was conquered by Joshua and the Israelites when they entered the Promised Land. The Israelites built at least six fortress cities on the eastern end of the larger Canaanite *tel* over a period of 350 years. Each was destroyed by Israel's enemies. The reconstructed fortress shown here probably dates to the time of Hezekiah. Arad is special because it contains the only Israelite temple ever discovered in archaeology—a temple active while Solomon's temple stood in Jerusalem. Imagine Israelite people coming to this small town to worship the same God worshiped in churches today.

Overhead Transparency 29. Panorama of the Temple at Arad. Locate the courts: (1) the outer (worship) court; (2) the holy place (priests' court); and (3) the Holy of Holies. NOTE: It might be helpful to compare this overhead transparency with Overhead Transparencies 30, 31, and 32 below and Overhead Transparency 12 ("The Temple at Arad") in this lesson.

Overhead Transparency 30. The Outer Court of the Temple at Arad. Locate the altar of sacrifice. It measures 4.5 feet high and 7.5 feet square, the same dimensions as the altar of the tabernacle (Exodus 27:1). It is made of unworked stones, just as God commanded (Exodus 20:25). A large stone on top provided a place for the sacrifice to be made. Archaeologists originally found a plastered channel on top of the altar to catch blood and direct it to the edge of the altar, where it could be collected. Some scholars believe that there was a metal rack on the stone to hold the meat of the sacrifice. If so, it has not survived.

This ancient structure provides the most basic elements of our relationship with God. Because of our sins, we are made right with God through the shedding of blood. Because of God's forgiveness, we "offer" our lives as sacrifices to Him.

Ask your students to read the following passages and answer the questions:

- 1 Corinthians 5:7. How does this altar point to Jesus? Imagine the members of the Arad community standing around the altar, 700 years before Jesus, seeking God's forgiveness and giving testimony that the animal blood pointed to the coming of the Messiah. What will you say to the citizens of Arad when you meet them in heaven?

- Romans 12:1. When the temple at Jerusalem was destroyed (both the first temple [586 B.C.] and the second temple [A.D. 70]), the Jewish followers of Yahweh pointed to passages like Micah 6:6–8 to indicate that obedience to God is the "new" sacrifice. How is that similar to Romans 12:1? How do you offer yourself as a "living sacrifice"?

Locate the base for the Bronze Sea. According to God's instructions for the tabernacle (Exodus 30:17–21 and 38:8) and Solomon's construction of the temple (2 Chronicles 4:2–5), the Bronze Sea was to stand in the outer court. This basin symbolized (1) the removal of ceremonial uncleanness before the sacrifice was offered and (2) the forgiveness resulting from the sacrifice itself. The Bronze Sea was not found at Arad. Possibly, it was made of metal and therefore too valuable to bury with the temple.

Ask your students to read the following passages and answer the questions:

- Acts 22:16 and 1 Corinthians 6:11. How is the laver related to Jesus' sacrifice? To the meaning of baptism?

Overhead Transparency 31. The Holy Place of the Temple at Arad. This room was the priests' court, which contained several key elements of the worship of Yahweh. Unseen just inside the opening is a stone bench, and across from the bench are the two incense altars at the entrance to the Holy of Holies. The bench may correspond to the table of showbread, or at least illustrate its location. We do not know why there are two altars here when there was only one in the tabernacle and the temple at Jerusalem. No golden lampstand was found in the excavations.

The term *showbread* could also mean "the bread of the Presence," because it was placed as an offering in the presence of God (Leviticus 24:5–9). This offering symbolized a thanksgiving gift to God, as well as a request for God's provision of food. The priests, on behalf of the people, ate the bread as a symbol of their relationship with God. Ask your students to respond to the following questions:

1. How do you place "bread" before God as a thank offering?
2. How does this relate to the Lord's Prayer (e.g., "Give us our daily bread")?
3. What do you do to illustrate your friendship and fellowship with God?

Overhead Transparency 32. The Holy of Holies of the Temple at Arad. The Holy of Holies was reached by climbing two steps. This provided the symbolism of going up to God that is so central to the biblical idea of worship. In this small room were two standing stones. Scholars debate whether these stones represented the acts of God (Genesis 28:18, Exodus 24:4, and Joshua 4:9) or the tablets of the Ten Commandments. Though only one stone was found standing, the clear parallels of this temple to Solomon's, the evidence of the worship of Yahweh, and the stones' location in the Holy of Holies leave little doubt that they did represent the Ten Commandments—God's covenant with Israel. The table of showbread (stone bench) and the altars of incense can be seen in the foreground at the entrance to the Holy of Holies.

Ask your students to respond to the following question: How do these tablets help you to visualize the Ten Commandments?

4. Guided Discussion: God's Covenant with Israel

The covenant God made with Israel through Moses on Mount Sinai is recorded in the Torah, the first five books of the Bible. It resembles the covenant form made between a greater party and a lesser party common in the biblical world. Probably, God used a covenant pattern familiar to the Israelites to help them understand the nature of the relationship He wanted with them.

a. Have your students read the following passages:

- Exodus 19:3–6—God promised the Israelites that they would be His people if they obeyed Him.
- Exodus 24:1–8—The people promised to do what the Lord said, and Moses sealed the covenant by sprinkling blood on the people.

- Exodus 24:12—God told Moses He would give him the Ten Commandments, the summary of God's covenant with Israel.

- Exodus 31:18—God gave Moses the two tablets of the Ten Commandments.

- Exodus 40:20–21—Moses placed the Ten Commandments in Israel's sacred place, the ark of the covenant.

b. Remind your students of the covenant format:

- A covenant contained the history leading to its establishment, the names of the parties involved, their responsibilities to each other, the rewards for upholding the covenant, the penalties incurred if it was broken, and the ceremonies that established it.

- A standard summary of the covenant was written, listing its key elements.

- Two copies of the covenant summary were made. One was placed in the sacred place of the greater party, and one in the sacred place of the lesser party. (The sacred place was often a temple or shrine.)

- The summary copies were regularly taken out and read. They did not express the entirety of the covenant but were symbolic of the whole document (much as wedding vows *represent* the total commitment of the bride and groom). Reading the covenant summary reminded the parties that a relationship, with all its elements (written and unwritten), existed between them.

c. Ask your students how the above information helps them to understand the following passages:

- Exodus 40:20–21, 25:22, 26:33, 30:6, 31:7; and Joshua 4:16. (*Testimony* is another word for *covenant.*) Why were the tablets put into the ark?

- Deuteronomy 31:10–13. When was the covenant to be read? Why was it read? The Ten Commandments are a summary of God's love for His people. Certainly, they are a list of dos and don'ts, but they are also much more. They are a guarantee that God loves us, and they should be read as if they were wedding vows, not a checklist.

- Exodus 32:15–16. What was written on the tablets? Traditionally, Christians have believed in two tablets of the law. One tablet (commandments 1–4) describes what our relationship with God should be; the other (commandments 5–10) describes what our relationship with other members of God's covenant should be. It is correct to divide the commandments into these two categories. Unfortunately, we have assumed (as have most Christian artists—just check the stained glass windows in any church) that God wrote four commandments on one tablet and six on the other. There is nothing in the Scriptures to support this idea. It would not have taken much space to write the Ten Commandments. Everything we know about Israelite culture points to *all 10 commandments being listed on each tablet.* God gave both copies to Moses because God's sacred place and Moses' sacred place were the same: the ark of the covenant.

    Ask your students to respond to the following questions:

    1. What do you think Moses thought when God gave him both copies?

    2. How important is it to God to be near His people?

    3. How does He accomplish that today? (See 1 Corinthians 3:16–17.)

OPTIONAL — Digging Deeper IV: God's Dwelling Place *(27–34 minutes)*

A. Guided Discussion: The Ark Signified God's Presence

In the Bible, God's presence is directly related to the role of the ark of the covenant and the Holy of Holies in the temple. Ask your students to read and summarize each of the following passages:

- Genesis 3:8. How near to His creation was God?

- Genesis 3:24. What was the result of sin?

- Genesis 11:5. Where is God in relation to His world? (NOTE: The Lord appeared or spoke to Abraham about a dozen times and to Moses more than 50 times.)

- Exodus 25:22. What was the purpose of the ark? (See also Exodus 40:34–35.)

- 2 Chronicles 5:7 and 7:1–3. What was one main purpose of the temple?

- Ezekiel 10:18–19. What happened to the presence of God because of Israel's unbelief?

- John 1:1,14. How did God restore His presence among His people?

- Acts 1:9. Where is Jesus today? (See also Ephesians 1:20–21.)

- 1 Corinthians 3:16–17. Where is the presence of God today?

B. Guided Discussion: We Are God's Dwelling Place

Ask your students to reflect on the following statements and respond to the questions:

- We are to our world what the ark and the temple were to Israel: Almighty God's dwelling place. What are the implications for the way we should live? God wants others to watch us so *that the world may know that He is God.*

- Why did the presence of God leave Israel? What does that mean for you today? For the church?

- If our secular culture is to know the presence of God, where will it see Him? How can you more effectively present the reality of God to others?

C. Personal Application

Ask your students to list three specific actions they can take to make God more real to those around them. If they feel comfortable doing so, they can relate their answers to the class. Spend a few moments in prayer, asking God to bless these plans of action.

5. Guided Discussion: What It Means to Be God's Temple

Have your students read the handout "The Ark of God" and then (individually or in small groups) consider the following questions:

a. Read Joshua 3:1–6,14–17 and Joshua 6:6–11. What did it mean for the ark of the covenant to go ahead of the army? How does this relate to our actions as Christians today?

b. Read 1 Samuel 4:1–11. Why didn't the ark produce the desired result in this battle? (Could it be that the wickedness of the people stood in the way of God's blessing?) Compare this with 1 Samuel 2:27–36. Can you apply this to our situation as Christians in Western culture? Do you think God will use us or work through us if we are guilty of the same sins as the culture we seek to influence for Him? Why or why not?

c. The ark represented the presence of God and was often the means by which God revealed Himself to His people (Exodus 25:17–22). According to 1 Corinthians 3:16–17, where does God choose to reveal Himself today? What does it mean to you to be the temple of the Holy Spirit? Specifically, how should it affect the things you do, the way you act, and the way you relate to unbelievers?

* * * * * * * * * *

Step Three: "The Blood Path"
(Genesis 15)

1. Lecture: Why Did the Israelites Shed Blood?

The central act of worship for the Israelites was the shedding of blood. Primitive as that may seem, God established and continually strengthened His relationship with His people through the ritual of animal sacrifice. Without a doubt, the writers of the New Testament believed that all the sacrifices pointed to, and were fulfilled by, Jesus Christ. In Hebrews 9:11–14, this belief is made clear. But what did the people of the Old Testament think of all that bloodshed? Did Abraham and Sarah understand that the sacrifices pointed to the Messiah? Did the priests of the tabernacle and the temple understand? No one knows for sure how much the Israelites knew. But one passage of the Old Testament, Genesis 15, gives insight into God's instruction to His people through the sacrifice system. Understanding this passage in its cultural setting reveals the details of the sacrificial system and the meaning of Jesus' atoning death.

2. Map Study: Hebron and Arad

Using the overhead transparency "Israel," locate Hebron (Mamre) for your students. Point out its proximity to Arad, where the video *God with Us* was filmed. Ask your students to read Genesis 13:18 and 14:13.

3. Guided Discussion: God's Willingness to Pay the Price

Ask your students to open their Bibles to Genesis 15. Read each verse, and have the students (individually or in small groups) answer the appropriate questions.

Verse 1: In what form did God come to Abram? What was God's promise to him?

Verse 2: What was Abram's reaction? Do you dare speak so directly (respectfully, of course) to God? Should you?

Verse 3: What was Abram's concern?

Verse 4: What was God's response?

Verse 5: What was the sign of God's promise?

Verse 6: What was Abram's response? God's reaction to Abram's faith? Would God react to your faith the same way today? How might you indicate that you are willing to take God at His word?

Verse 7: What did God recall from the past? Why did this establish God's right to make a covenant with Abram? (See the handout "A Covenant Guarantee.")

Verse 8:   What was Abram's reaction? Again, note his directness. Put Abram's reaction in your own words (e.g., "Prove it!").

Verse 9:   How did God react to Abram's request for proof? What is a heifer? How do you know that the ram was not a goat?

Verse 10:   What did Abram do after he got the animals? How does this show you that he knew what was happening? NOTE: This ceremony was practiced by the culture and so was known to Abram. The animals were arranged so that the blood ran to the middle of the altar, forming a pool or path of blood between the two parties. Both parties, beginning with the greater one, would then walk through the "blood path" as a symbol of what would happen if they did not keep their word. This type of ceremony is called a self-maledictory oath: "May this be done to me if I break my word."

Verses 13–16: What did God promise?

Verse 17:   What symbols passed between the pieces? How do you know that God was symbolized? What was God saying? From Abram's perspective, could God have broken the covenant? How do you know a covenant was made? (See verse 18.)

Notice the symbols that passed between the pieces: a smoking firepot and a blazing torch. When was fire a symbol of God (Exodus 2:2 and Acts 2:3)? When was smoke a symbol of God (Exodus 19:18 and Isaiah 6:4)?

With these two symbols, God made a covenant with Abram, which meant that Abram also was expected to put his life on the line for his obedience. That may explain the "thick and dreadful darkness" that came over Abram earlier that night (verse 12). If so, the image of this passage is God's willingness to pay the price for His own breaking of the covenant (which could not happen to a perfect God). The story also shows God's willingness to pay the price for Abram's (and his descendants') failure to keep the covenant.

Ask a student to read aloud Genesis 17:1–2. Then ask your students to answer the following questions:

1. In confirming the covenant (already made in chapter 15), what was Abram's responsibility (not mentioned in chapter 15)? Who was this covenant with? Could Abram and his descendants keep this covenant? By walking the blood path for Abram and his descendants, what was God promising? What does this have to do with Jesus?

2. How would God's walking the blood path help the Israelites understand the meaning of their sacrifices? Could the sacrifices have been reminders of God's promise to pay with His own life for breaking the covenant?

3. What does it mean to you that God was willing to pay the price for your sins? If you desire, relate your response to the class.

4. How does the realization of God's forgiveness help us to be His instruments to those around us? Think of a time when sin or guilt prevented you from being a witness. If you feel comfortable doing so, relate your example to the class.

4. Guided Discussion: Preparing for Jesus' Coming

How do each of the following items provide a background for Jesus' coming?

*   the tabernacle/temple/ark of the covenant (Answer: the presence of God)

*   God's covenant with Abram (Answer: the promise of God)

*   the tablets of the Ten Commandments (Answer: the relationship with God)

The next set of lessons in this series begins with the New Testament and God's great act of fulfillment: the birth of Jesus.

Conclusion

God began restoring His presence among His people in the symbolism of the tabernacle, the temple, and the ark of the covenant. He declared His commitment to the Israelites by walking the blood path to make a covenant with Abraham and his descendants. He reinforced that commitment through regular sacrifices on the altar. But all of this, though a spectacular demonstration of God's love, anticipated an even greater act of love: the birth of God's own Son.

The person of Jesus was to be the fulfillment or completion of everything that came before. God would walk with His people as He had with Adam and Eve. The blood of Jesus the Lamb would atone for the sins of those who believed in Him. In Jesus, God reaffirms His dedication to the covenant relationship that His servant Abraham had experienced.

Jesus' ministry is the subject of the next set of lessons. Don't miss the ending!

A COVENANT GUARANTEE

Lesson Ten

Handout #1

God created human beings with the ability, even the deep need, to be in relationship with Him. When Adam and Eve sinned, they broke the friendship between God and His creatures. So God developed a plan of salvation that would restore His children to Himself. To help them understand the depth of His love and commitment, God chose to seal the relationship with a familiar cultural form: the covenant.

A COVENANT IS A RELATIONSHIP

The people of the Bible understood covenants well. In fact, they made covenants daily to define and describe their relationships with each other. Abraham made a covenant with the Philistine king Abimelech to resolve their conflict over a water source (Genesis 21:22–34). David and Jonathan made a covenant that established their everlasting friendship and that affirmed David's right to the throne of Israel (1 Samuel 18:3 and 23:18). Jacob and Laban, his father-in-law, made a covenant in which each promised never to harm the other and Jacob promised to provide for Laban's daughters (Genesis 31:43–53).

The fundamental difference between covenants and other agreements is the *relationship* established between the covenant makers. Each party made specific promises and could expect certain benefits (and penalties, if the promises were broken) based on the terms of the covenant. But this relationship went far beyond legal concepts. Covenanted parties viewed each other as friends who were bound together permanently. Abraham's covenant with Abimelech allowed these two very different men to live peaceably in the same area (Genesis 21:34). The covenant between David and Jonathan was one of mutual loyalty and love (1 Samuel 18:3). The legal obligations of a covenant relationship were based on the friendship established by the covenant itself. To be in covenant was to be in relationship.

Covenants were made before witnesses—sometimes things (Genesis 31:52), sometimes God Himself (Genesis 31:53). Often, symbols were used to remind the parties of the obligations and benefits established by the covenants. Jacob erected standing stones as a reminder of his relationship with Laban (Genesis 31:45–46,52). God sealed His covenant (His promise to never destroy the earth with another flood) with Noah by placing a rainbow in the sky for everyone to see.

A COVENANT IS "CUT," NOT MADE

Though our biblical translations refer to people "making" a covenant, the Hebrews described the establishment of this type of relationship as "cutting" a covenant.

The cutting, symbolized by the slaughter of animals (Exodus 24:5,8), indicated that each person in the covenant promised to give his or her own life to keep its terms. To break a covenant was to invite one's own death as a penalty. There are no more serious relationships than those that are a commitment of life itself.

Thus God's use of covenants to describe His relationship with His people (Genesis 15; Hebrews 13:20–21) is striking for several reasons. It shows that God wanted to bond eternally with a people who persistently rejected Him. It shows that God was willing to prove His devotion to the relationship by offering His own life. Finally, and probably most stunning of all, it shows that God not only was willing to offer His own life to keep the covenant, but He also was willing to pay the price for any covenant failure on the part of the human beings with whom He was in relationship. This promise certainly exceeded the limits of human covenant-making practices.

UNEQUAL COVENANTS

Many of the human covenants in the Bible are between equals. Marriage is such a relationship (Malachi 2:14). In the culture of the ancient Near East, there were also covenants between unequal parties. These relationships were defined and established by the superior party and could not be changed by the lesser party, such as when great kings made treaties with conquered kings who became vassals. The lesser party could either accept the offer of relationship or reject it and exist in conflict with the greater party.

COVENANT FORMS

Ancient Near Eastern covenants, especially those between unequal parties, were complex relationships. There were many factors that had to be considered—for example, the right of the greater party to make the covenant, the obligations of each party, the penalties and benefits of the relationship, and the history of the relationship. Because of the large number of issues involved, covenant documents were usually quite long. God's covenant with Israel through Moses is recorded in the Torah, the first five books of the Bible. God's covenant with us in Jesus is described in all 66 books of the Bible.

Because of the length of covenants, a certain pattern was followed so that people could make sense of them. This pattern governed the material contained in a covenant, including its content and form. A summary document representing the entirety of the relationship and following the accepted form of a covenant document was also provided. If the Torah is God's covenant with Israel, the Ten Commandments, inscribed on stone tablets, are a summary document.

We must be careful to recognize that there are many covenant forms and that God does not always use existing practices (which He caused to develop anyway) in dealing with His people. But once we understand what a covenant relationship meant and how it was established, we will realize the extent of God's love for us and His desire to restore the relationship sin destroyed. Keeping in mind that God cut covenants as the superior party so He alone determined their content, let's briefly review the components of the covenant God made with the Hebrews.

In general, ancient Near Eastern covenants had five sections:

1. The Preamble

This section identified the two parties of the covenant. In the Torah, God established the identities of the parties in the creation story. He was the Creator, and Israel was His creation. In the covenant summary, the Ten Commandments, He said simply, "I am the LORD your God" (Exodus 20:2).

2. The Historical Prologue

In this part of the document, the history leading to the cutting of the covenant was recited to prove the right of the superior party to make it. In the Torah, the stories of the Fall, Noah, Abraham, and the Exodus are detailed as the basis for God's making the covenant with Moses on Mount Sinai. In the Ten Commandments, the summary is simply, ". . . who brought you out of Egypt, out of the land of slavery" (Exodus 20:2).

3. Requirements (Commandments)

The Torah contains 613 of the requirements God placed on the people with whom He was in relationship. The number of obligations He placed on Himself was even greater. In the summary of the commandments, these requirements were simplified to 10 (Exodus 20:3–17). Some scholars have noted that Jesus reduced His summary even further, to just two (Matthew 22:37–40).

4. Blessings and Curses

Keeping a covenant brought specific rewards, and breaking a covenant brought specific penalties. In the Torah, such blessings and curses are many and varied. Moses summarized both in Deuteronomy 28 in a powerful challenge to the Israelites. The summary document also contains curses and blessings scattered throughout the discussion of the requirements (see, e.g., Exodus 20:5,7 for curses, and Exodus 20:6,12 for blessings).

5. The Summary Document

The summary document served two purposes. Because it was short, it could be easily read and stored. Because it summarized the entire covenant, it represented the total relationship between the parties. Normally, two copies of this document were made, and each party would take a copy and put it in a sacred place for safekeeping.

Because the Bible is silent about what was written on each tablet of the Ten Commandments, and because the culture demanded that two identical copies of a covenant always be made, it seems clear that each tablet contained all 10 commandments. One copy was God's, and the other belonged to the people of Israel.

Thus when God gave both tablets to Moses, He was making a profound statement. Since God trusted Moses with His copy of the covenant, it indicated that His sacred place was the same as Israel's: the ark of the covenant in the Holy of Holies in the tabernacle.

PRESERVING A COVENANT

A covenant was carefully recorded and preserved. It was to be read regularly and obeyed always. Moses wrote down the words of God's covenant with

His people in the Torah and commanded that it be read every seven years (Deuteronomy 31:9–13,24–26). The summary document, the Ten Commandments, was stored in the most sacred place: the ark of the covenant, God's earthly throne.

CONCLUSION

The Ten Commandments were God's covenant with Israel, and they are His covenant with us today. To read the commandments is to learn God's will for human society. It is important to remember that the commandments, as a summary document, represent the total covenant—the total *relationship*—between God and His people. To read them is far more than to review a checklist of God's requirements. It is to hear God say, "I am God, and I love you enough to make a covenant (be in relationship) with you through My own blood."

It is only in the person of Jesus that we can fully understand this love. In Christ, God fulfilled the promise He made to the Hebrews of giving His own life to seal the covenant He had made with them. For this reason, Jesus could say, "Do not think that I have come to abolish the Law or the Prophets; I have not come to abolish them but to fulfill them" (Matthew 5:17).

God's choice of the covenant to describe His relationship with His people highlights the degree of His love for us. Not only does the great sovereign Creator of heaven and earth descend to be in relationship with sinful human beings, but He offers His own life to provide escape for covenant breakers. Understanding what a covenant was in ancient Near Eastern culture made relationship with God an indescribable gift to those who believed in Him.

It should be no less for us.

THE ARK OF GOD

God spoke to His people through their culture. He used their language and their customs. He described Himself as a shepherd, for example, an occupation they knew well. When God commanded the Hebrews to build the tabernacle and temple, the builders followed cultural patterns that had been known for centuries. And long before God gave Moses the Ten Commandments, ancient peoples used tablets as symbols and summaries of covenants.

The ark of the covenant, however, was unique in the history of the Near East.

THE DESIGN

The specific design for the ark is given in Exodus 25:10–22. Its role was so important to God that He described its construction before any other sacred object, even before the tabernacle itself. It was made of acacia wood, an extremely hard wood common to the Sinai Peninsula. The ark was 3 feet 9 inches long, 2 feet 3 inches wide, and 2 feet 3 inches high. It was plated with gold and had a gold rim around the top. It stood on four legs, and on each side were two gold rings so poles could be inserted for the Levites, the priestly tribe, to carry it. The cover, called the mercy seat or atonement seat, was pure gold. On the top of the lid were two cherubim—probably sphinxes with their wings stretched over the cover.

WHAT THE ARK MEANT TO GOD'S PEOPLE

The ark became the focus of God's presence among His people. God would regularly appear in a cloud of glory on the mercy seat of the ark (Exodus 25:22). On the Day of Atonement (Yom Kippur), the great holy day of the Bible, the high priest would enter the Holy of Holies chamber in front of the ark, and God would appear in the cloud over the cover (Leviticus 16:2). A person who came before the ark was entering into God's presence.

The image of the cherubim on the cover of the ark expressed the people's longing to feel safe in God's sheltering arms: ". . . under his wings you will find refuge" (Psalm 91:4). The ark provided evidence that the holy God of Abraham was a protecting, forgiving presence in the lives of His people.

The ark also gave assurance that the Lord was sovereign over all things. The people saw the box as God's footstool (1 Chronicles 28:2). "The LORD reigns, let the nations tremble; he sits enthroned between the cherubim, let the earth shake" (Psalm 99:1). What was there to fear when God was on His throne attended by the cherubim?

THE COVENANT

The ark's central purpose was to hold the Ten Commandments (Exodus 25:16), the summary of God's covenant with His people. The covenant itself comprised the Torah, the first five books of the Bible. Following ancient Near Eastern custom, God instructed Moses to make two summary documents of the covenant as His guarantee that His word would never fail. Normally, each of the covenanted parties took a summary copy and put it in his most sacred place to read regularly as a reminder of the covenant. Apparently, God made the two summary copies (each containing all 10 commandments) and gave them both to Moses, ordering him to place them in the ark.

Imagine Moses' reaction when he learned that the most sacred place for God and for Israel was the same—the ark! As the ark was the presence of God to Israel, so Jesus became the presence of God during His ministry . . . but that's another story.

The ark of the covenant, the symbol of God's presence,
led the Israelites into the Promised Land.

GLOSSARY

Aegean Sea: Body of water east of Greece dotted with many islands. Scholars believe the Philistines came from this area.

Ai: City near Bethel, north of Jerusalem, that God helped Israel destroy. It controlled the approach to the mountain range from the east.

Aijalon Valley: Valley connecting the coastal plain and the Judea Mountains where God made the sun stand still for Joshua.

altar of incense: Located in the holy place or priests' room of the tabernacle or temple, just outside the Holy of Holies. The altar was 1.5 feet square and 3 feet high. The incense symbolized the "sweet smell" of the worshipers' prayers going up to God.

altar of sacrifice: Structure used for presenting sacrifices to God. A large altar of sacrifice (30 feet by 30 feet and 15 feet high) stood in the outer court of the temple at Jerusalem (as it had in the tabernacle). It symbolically stood before God's presence to indicate the need for forgiveness before approaching God.

Arad: Town 17 miles north of Beersheba at the edge of the Negev and the Hebron Mountains. It was an important fortress city that protected the southern approaches to Jerusalem.

ark of the covenant: The Hebrew word means "box" or "chest." It contained the tablets of the Ten Commandments. The cover represented God's throne.

Armageddon: Transliteration of the Hebrew *har megiddon*, which means literally the "hill (or mountain) of Megiddo." Revelation 16:16 uses this place to symbolize the final great battle between good and evil. Many battles were fought at this location because the main trade route went through a mountain pass nearby. *See also* **Valley of Jezreel**.

Ashdod: Philistine city-state on the Mediterranean Sea.

Ashkelon: Philistine city-state on the Mediterranean Sea and the international trade route Via Maris.

Ashtoreth (plural: Ashteroth): Canaanite goddess of fertility and love. She is thought to be the daughter of the fertility goddess Asherah.

Assyria: Nation in Mesopotamia that became a large empire in the time of the kings of Israel and Judah. Its capital was Nineveh. The Assyrians were extremely cruel, and God used them to punish the northern kingdom for its Baal worship.

atonement seat: Slab of gold on top of the ark of the covenant on which the golden cherubim stood. It symbolized God's throne.

Azekah: Small city above the Elah Valley where David fought Goliath.

Baal: Canaanite god of fertility. He is often portrayed as the god of storms, lightning, thunder, and rain. He was worshiped in horrible ways. The name means "lord" or "master." Israel was seduced into worshiping him.

bedouins: Nomads who live mainly in the wilderness areas of the Middle East. They speak Arabic and are generally Muslim. They retain a lifestyle much like that of the early biblical characters Abraham, Isaac, and Jacob.

Beelzebub: Corruption of the word *Beelzebul* ("Prince Baal"), meaning "lord of the flies." It was used by Jesus to refer to the prince of demons, the devil.

Beelzebul: Philistine god worshiped at Ekron. It means "Prince Baal."

Beersheba: City in the central Negev. It was settled before 3000 B.C. Abraham and Isaac lived here. Abraham gave it the name *Beersheba*, which means "well of the oath" or "well of the seven" (Genesis 21:33). Often used to refer to the southern end of the Promised Land.

Beth Horon: Two cities (Upper and Lower Beth Horon) guarding the Beth Horon pass. The main west-east road from the coastal plain into the mountains to Jericho went through this pass. Here God made the sun stand still for Joshua.

Beth Shean: City at the eastern entrance to the Valley of Jezreel. The Philistines hung Saul's and Jonathan's bodies from its walls.

Beth Shemesh: City in the Soreq Valley near where Samson lived. The Philistines returned the ark of the covenant here.

Bronze Sea: Bronze basin at the entrance to the tabernacle used for ceremonial purification before sacrifices were made. It also symbolized God's forgiveness after sacrifices were made. Solomon commissioned a large basin for the temple at Jerusalem. It was over 14 feet in diameter and seven feet high; it weighed over 25 tons and held 13,000 gallons of water. It sat on the backs of 12 oxen, three facing north, three facing west, three facing south, and three facing east.

Canaan: Old Testament name for the Promised Land. It means "land of purple," referring to the color of the dye produced from shellfish along Canaan's coast.

Canaanite: The word originally meant "merchant" or "trader." Eventually, it came to refer to the people of the region.

central mountains: Region made up of three mountain ranges: Samaria in the north, Judea in the middle, and Hebron in the south.

cherem: To devote something or someone totally to God, often through destruction.

Chorazin: City just north of the Sea of Galilee where Jesus performed many miracles. Jesus condemned the city for its unbelief.

coastal plain: Flat, fertile area of Israel along the Mediterranean Sea that comprises the Plain of Sharon in the north and Philistine territory in the south.

Dagon: Philistine god. Recent evidence indicates that he was the grain god believed to be responsible for fertility.

Dan: One of the 12 Hebrew tribes originally placed between the Philistines and Judah. They migrated north and established the city of Dan as the northern border of Israel.

Dead Sea: Lowest, saltiest body of water in the world. Located in the Great Rift Valley, this sea is 10 miles wide and 50 miles long.

Dome of the Rock: The Muslim mosque (Mosque of Omar) built in the seventh century on the Temple Mount. The presence of this mosque makes it impossible to excavate the Mount.

Eastern Gate: Main eastern entrance to the temple area in Jerusalem. In some traditions, it is believed to be the location of the Last Judgment. Also known as the Beautiful Gate.

Ekron: One of the five Philistine city-states, it is the one closest to the Judea Mountains.

Elah Valley: Valley in the Shephelah between the coastal plain and the Judea Mountains. David fought Goliath here.

En-Gedi (also En Gedi): Oasis near the Dead Sea in the middle of the Judea Wilderness. David hid from Saul here.

Eshtaol: Small town on the hills above the Soreq Valley, near Samson's birthplace.

Essenes: Members of a Jewish religious movement, probably an offshoot of the Sadducees, that began about 200 B.C. in reaction to the secularization of the priesthood. Authors of the Dead Sea Scrolls, the Essenes lived in the wilderness, waiting for the imminent arrival of the Messiah. They had much in common with early Christians.

firstfruits: The first part of the produce of Israelite farmers that belonged to God.

First Jewish Revolt: Revolt against Rome by the Jewish people that resulted in the destruction of the temple and Jerusalem in A.D. 70.

Gath: One of the five Philistine city-states. Goliath was born here.

Gaza: One of the five Philistine city-states. Samson died here.

Gezer: One of the cities that controlled the international trade route Via Maris. It was near the coastal plain and the Aijalon Valley.

Gilead Mountains: Mountains east of the Jordan Valley between the Dead Sea and the Sea of Galilee.

Gomorrah: City near the southern end of the Dead Sea that God destroyed because of its wickedness, which included oppression of the poor.

Great Rift Valley: Valley east of Israel where the Sea of Galilee and the Dead Sea are located. Also known as the Jordan Valley.

har: Hebrew for "hill" or "mountain."

Hazor: Major city in northern Israel and one of the key cities on the international trade route Via Maris. It was fortified by Solomon.

Hebron: City in the southern Judea Mountains 20 miles south of Jerusalem. Abraham lived near here and purchased a tomb, the cave of Machpelah, where he was buried with Sarah, Isaac, Rebekah, Jacob, and Leah.

high place: Elevated location used in the worship of gods. The God of the Bible also met His people in high places.

Hill of Moreh: Hill at the intersection of the Valley of Jezreel and the Valley of Harod. Gideon and 300 men defeated the Midianites, the desert people (bedouins), here. Also known as Mount Moreh.

Hinnom (Hebrew: *ge-hinnom*; Greek: *gehenna*): Valley to the west of Jerusalem that was at one time the city sewage dump and the place where Judean kings sacrificed their children. This valley, with its filth, rottenness, and burning flesh, came to symbolize hell.

Holy of Holies: Inner part of the tabernacle and/or temple where the ark of the covenant was placed. It symbolized God's dwelling place.

Jericho: Located in an oasis near the Dead Sea, this city guards the entrance to Israel from the east. It was destroyed by Joshua. Because it was devoted to God as the firstfruits of the land, it was never to be rebuilt. Ahab disobeyed this command.

Jerusalem: City built on Mount Moriah, where Abraham offered Isaac to God. David made it the religious and political center of Israel.

Jezreel: City guarding the Valley of Harod and the route from the Valley of Jezreel to Beth Shean. Here Ahab and Jezebel had a summer palace, Ahab stole Naboth's vineyard, and Jezebel was killed.

Joppa: This Old Testament port city is on the coast of the Mediterranean Sea. Jonah sailed from here.

Jordan River: Largest river in Israel. It flows from Mount Hermon to the Dead Sea. In the Bible, it symbolized a barrier to be crossed.

Jordan Valley. *See* **Great Rift Valley.**

Judah: Fourth son of Jacob from whom the tribe of Judah and Jesus descended. Also the name of the southern kingdom after Israel divided in 926 B.C.

Judea: New Testament name for the Promised Land after the Babylonian Captivity (586 B.C.). Originally, it referred to the area that belonged to the tribe of Judah.

Judea Wilderness: Area from the eastern slopes of the Judea Mountains down to the Great Rift Valley, from Jericho in the north to south of the Dead Sea. Little rain falls here, so there are few plants or animals. Many deep wadis penetrate this wilderness.

Kidron Valley: Deep wadi forming the eastern border of Jerusalem between David's City and the Mount of Olives. The spring of Gihon and the garden of Gethsemane are in this valley.

King's Highway: Major trade route east of the Jordan Valley. It was a more difficult road to travel than the international trade route Via Maris.

Lachish: Key city in the southern Shephelah. It was destroyed by the Assyrians during the reign of Hezekiah, and later by the Babylonians and Nebuchadnezzar.

massebah. See **standing stone.**

Mediterranean Sea: Known in the Bible as the Great Sea, it formed the western border of Israel. Since the Jews were not a seafaring people, the Mediterranean was more of a boundary than an integral part of their lives.

Megiddo: The most strategic city in Israel, it guarded a key mountain pass of the international trade route Via Maris. It was one of the cities that Solomon fortified. According to Revelation, it represents Armageddon, the final battle between God's people and the devil's followers. *See also* **Armageddon.**

mercy seat. *See* **atonement seat.**

Mesopotamia: Refers to the land between the Tigris and Euphrates Rivers, as well as the surrounding area. The patriarchs came from here. The empires of Assyria, Persia, and Babylon were here.

mezuzah: Hebrew for "doorpost." God's command to write His words "upon the doorframes of your houses" led to the practice of placing a small box containing verses from the Bible, also called a *mezuzah*, on the doorposts of Jewish homes.

Micmash (or Michmash): City north of Jerusalem that guarded one of the approaches from the coastal plain.

Middle East: Modern term referring to the area of Israel and the countries surrounding it.

Moab Mountains: Mountain range east of the Dead Sea where the nation of Moab lived.

Mount Carmel: Mountain ridge in Israel that divides the Valley of Jezreel from the coastal plain. Elijah confronted the prophets of Baal here.

Mount Ebal: Mountain near the city of Shechem where an altar to God was built. Joshua gave the curses of the covenant on this mountain (the blessings on Mount Gerizim) when he renewed the covenant after entering the Promised Land, as Moses had commanded him.

Mount Gerizim: Mountain near the city of Shechem where Joshua pronounced the covenant blessings (the curses on Mount Ebal) when he renewed the covenant after entering the Promised Land, as Moses had commanded him.

Mount Gilboa: Mountain on the southern edge of the Valley of Jezreel. Saul and Jonathan died here.

Mount Hermon: Mountain on the northern border of Israel. More than 9,000 feet above sea level, it is often covered with snow. Water from this mountain forms the Jordan River.

Mount Sedom (or Sodom): This mountain ridge at the southern end of the Dead Sea is composed of salt. It retains the name of the city of Sodom, which was probably nearby.

Mount Sinai: Mountain where God met Moses to establish His covenant with the Israelites. Here He gave the Ten Commandments and the instructions for the building of the tabernacle. Many scholars believe Sinai refers to Jebel Musa, a peak in the Sinai Peninsula, the area between the Red Sea and the Gulf of Aqaba. This peak is 7,500 feet high. Others put Mount Sinai further north; still others in Arabia.

Mount Tabor: Mountain at the northeast edge of the Valley of Jezreel. Site of the battle between Deborah and Barak and Jabin, king of Hazor.

murex shellfish: Shellfish found along the coast of the Mediterranean Sea north of Israel, where the Phoenicians lived. Purple dye was produced from these shellfish.

Nazareth: Small village just north of the Valley of Jezreel. Name means "branch" or "shoot." Jesus lived here during His childhood to fulfill the prophecy that he would be a Nazarene, a shoot from Jesse's stump (Isaiah 11:1).

Nazirite: Individual who showed his devotion to God by choosing to separate himself from other people through his lifestyle. He made a three-part vow: to never cut his hair or beard, to abstain from any grape product, and to avoid contact with anything dead. Samson was a Nazirite.

Near East: Ancient term referring to the area of Israel and the countries surrounding it, including Egypt and Mesopotamia.

Negev: Word means "dry" and/or "south" and refers to the wilderness in southern Israel.

northern kingdom: When Israel divided after Solomon's death (926 B.C.), the northern 10 tribes under Jeroboam became the northern kingdom, or Israel. The Assyrians destroyed them in 722 B.C.

Oholah: Nickname given by Ezekiel to the northern kingdom. It means "her tent" and probably refers to the Baal high places the northern kingdom built.

Oholibah: Nickname given by Ezekiel to the southern kingdom. It means "tent worshiper," a reference to the Baal worship of Judah.

Palestine: Name given to the Promised Land after the Second Jewish Revolt (A.D. 132–135). It derives from the word *Philistia* and was used by the Romans to denigrate the Jews.

Philistia: Means "land of the Philistines." It was on the fertile coastal plain.

Philistine: This cultured seafaring group from the Aegean moved into Israel at about the same time as the Israelites.

Phoenicia: Country along the Mediterranean Sea to the north of Israel. The people worshiped Baal in the same fertility cults as did the Canaanites. Jezebel came from here.

pool of Siloam: Pool created when Hezekiah ordered a tunnel dug from the spring of Gihon on the eastern side of the hill on which Jerusalem was built, to the western side within the city walls. It provided the city with water during the Assyrian siege.

Qumran: Archaeological site on the northwestern shore of the Dead Sea. Many scholars believe this area was the home of the Essenes, who wrote the Dead Sea Scrolls.

Samaria: Name of a city and region. The city was founded by Omri, king of Israel ca. 880 B.C., and Ahab built a magnificent palace there. Samaria became a center for Baal worship. It was destroyed by the Assyrians in 722 B.C. During Jesus' time, it was a district of Israel.

Samaria Mountains: Northern part of the central mountain range in Israel.

Sea of Galilee: Israel's largest freshwater lake is in the northern part of the country. It is 13 miles long and seven miles wide.

Second Jewish Revolt: In this revolt of A.D. 132–135, the Romans removed the nation of Israel. Also known as the Bar Kochba Revolt.

secular humanism: Modern worldview based on an evolutionary model that considers human beings the ultimate life form and denies the existence or relevance of God. Right and wrong are determined by human standards, not God's.

Shephelah: Hebrew for "lowlands." It refers to the area between the Judea Mountains and the coastal plain where the Israelites and Philistines met.

Siloam Inscription: After workers built the tunnel of Hezekiah, they carved a description of its creation in the stone roof. The inscription tells how two teams of workers, digging from opposite directions, met in the middle. It is unusual because the story is told from the perspective of the workers and not the king. It is in a museum in Istanbul, Turkey.

Sinai Peninsula: Peninsula south of Israel. Mount Sinai, where Moses received the Ten Commandments, may be located here. The Israelites wandered here for 40 years.

"sitting in the gate": Synonym for being a ruler, judge, or official, because the gate compartments functioned as courthouses.

Sodom: City near the southern end of the Dead Sea that was destroyed by God because of its wickedness, which included oppression of the poor.

Soreq (Sorek) Valley: Valley linking the coastal plain and the Judea Mountains through the Shephelah. Samson lived here.

southern kingdom: When Israel divided after Solomon's death (926 B.C.), the tribe of Judah under Rehoboam became the southern kingdom, or Judah. In 586 B.C., God punished the people for their sins by exiling them to Babylon for 70 years. Jesus was born into this tribe.

spring of Gihon: Spring in the Kidron Valley near Jerusalem. It was the main water source for the city during Old Testament times. Hezekiah built a tunnel that directed the spring's water inside the city walls. *Gihon* means "gushing out."

standing stone: Large stone erected as a testimony to a significant act of God (or gods). Standing stones could serve pagan as well as God-honoring purposes.

stele: Standing stone with an inscription. Our practice of placing tombstones over the graves of loved ones probably derives from this special standing stone.

syncretism: Combining different forms of belief or practice. The Israelites practiced syncretism when they tried to worship both God and Baal.

table of showbread: Table that stood in the holy place of the tabernacle and temple, outside the Holy of Holies. Priests placed the bread of the Presence (Exodus 25:30), or showbread, on it. The bread symbolized the Israelites' commitment to give the Lord the results of their work. It also testified that everything they received was a gift from God.

tel: Large mound or hill composed of layers of debris from several different periods of settlement.

Temple Mount: Refers to the platform on Mount Moriah and to the highest point on the mountain itself. The Mount was originally built by Solomon and later expanded by Herod.

topheth: Place where the Israelites sacrificed their children. Based on a Hebrew word meaning "furnace" or "fireplace," the word was altered by Hebrew scribes to mean "shameful thing." It came to apply as well to the cemetery where the victims' remains were buried and to the location in the Hinnom valley where the sacrifices occurred.

Torah: Hebrew word meaning "teaching" or "instruction." It refers to the first five books of Moses.

Valley of Armageddon. *See* **Valley of Jezreel.**

Valley of Jehoshaphat: Place where the Lord will summon the world to be judged. (*Jehoshaphat* means "the Lord will judge.") The Kidron Valley east of Jerusalem is believed to be this location.

Valley of Jezreel: Large, flat, fertile plain in northern Israel between the Galilee Mountains and the Samaria Mountains. The international trade route Via Maris passed through this area. It is also known as the Valley of Armageddon.

Via Maris: One name used for the international trade route that passed through Israel.

wadi (Hebrew: *nahal*): Arabic word that refers to a riverbed that is dry except during the rainy season, when it becomes a raging stream from runoff in distant mountains.

Wilderness of Paran: Wilderness south of the Judea and Negev mountains between the Wilderness of Zin and the Sinai Peninsula. The Israelites wandered here for 40 years.

Yeshua: Hebrew for *Jesus*, a contraction of the Old Testament *Joshua*. It means "Yahweh saves."

Ziklag: City in southern Judea controlled by the Philistines. Achish, king of the Philistine city of Gath, gave Ziklag to David before David became king of Israel. David used the city as a base to expand his power with the people of Judea.

Zorah: Town in the Shephelah where the tribe of Dan settled. Samson came from here.

APPENDIX

THE MIDDLE EASTERN WORLD

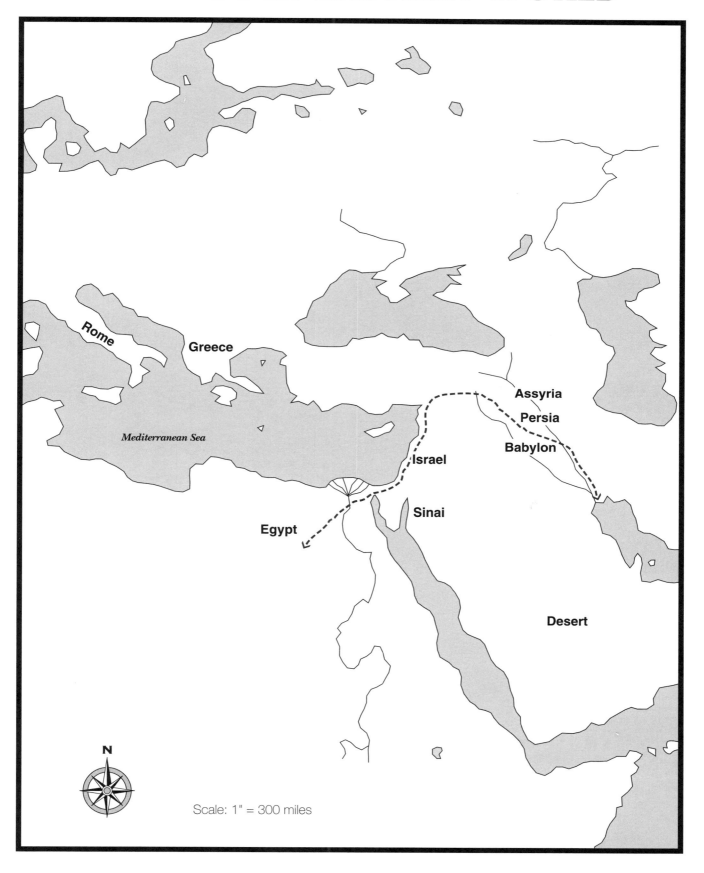

Rome

Greece

Assyria

Persia

Babylon

Mediterranean Sea

Israel

Sinai

Egypt

Desert

N

Scale: 1" = 300 miles

TOPOGRAPHY OF ISRAEL

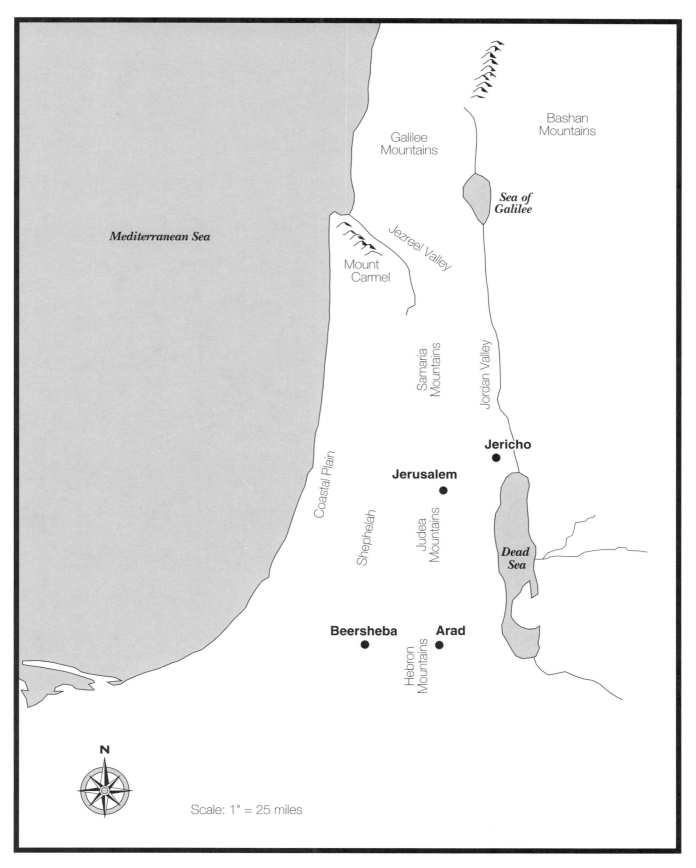

Bashan Mountains

Galilee Mountains

Sea of Galilee

Mediterranean Sea

Jezreel Valley

Mount Carmel

Samaria Mountains

Jordan Valley

Jericho

Jerusalem

Coastal Plain

Shephelah

Judea Mountains

Dead Sea

Beersheba   **Arad**

Hebron Mountains

N

Scale: 1" = 25 miles

THE VALLEY OF JEZREEL

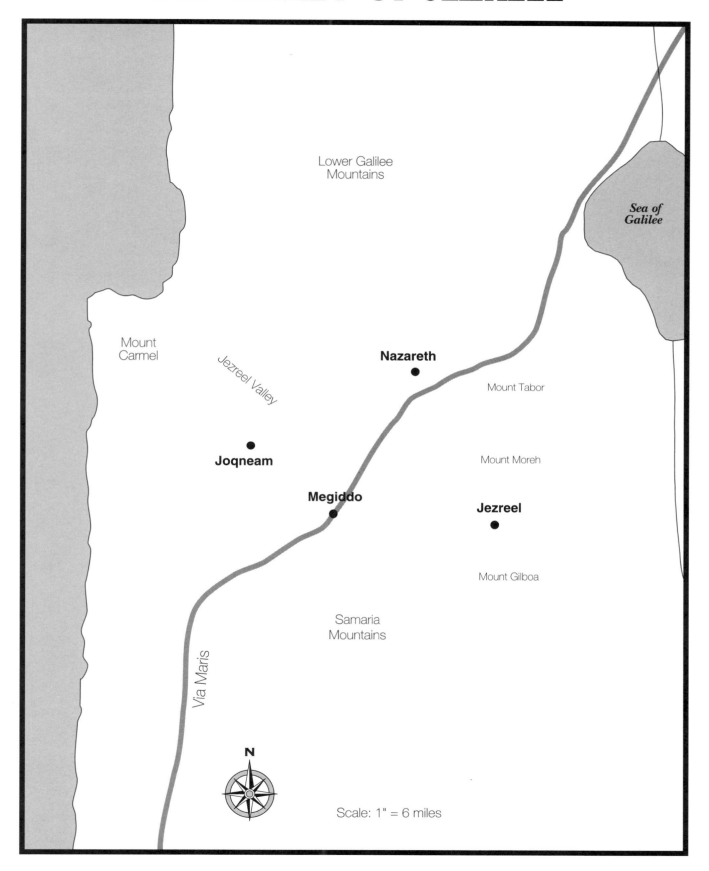

Lower Galilee
Mountains

Sea of
Galilee

Mount
Carmel

Jezreel Valley

Nazareth

Mount Tabor

Mount Moreh

Joqneam

Megiddo

Jezreel

Mount Gilboa

Samaria
Mountains

Via Maris

N

Scale: 1" = 6 miles

ISRAEL

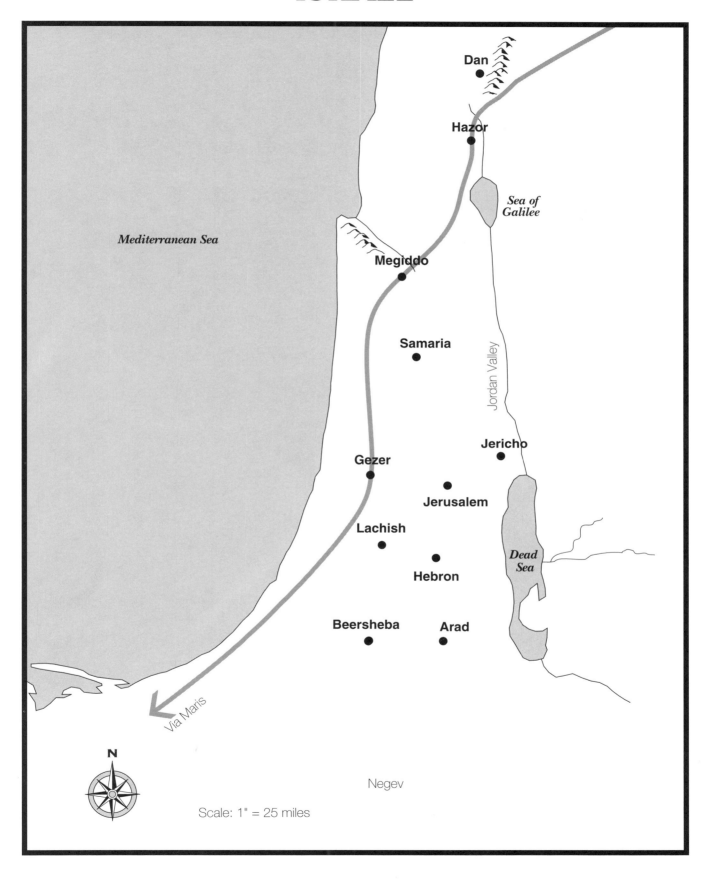

THE DIVIDED KINGDOM

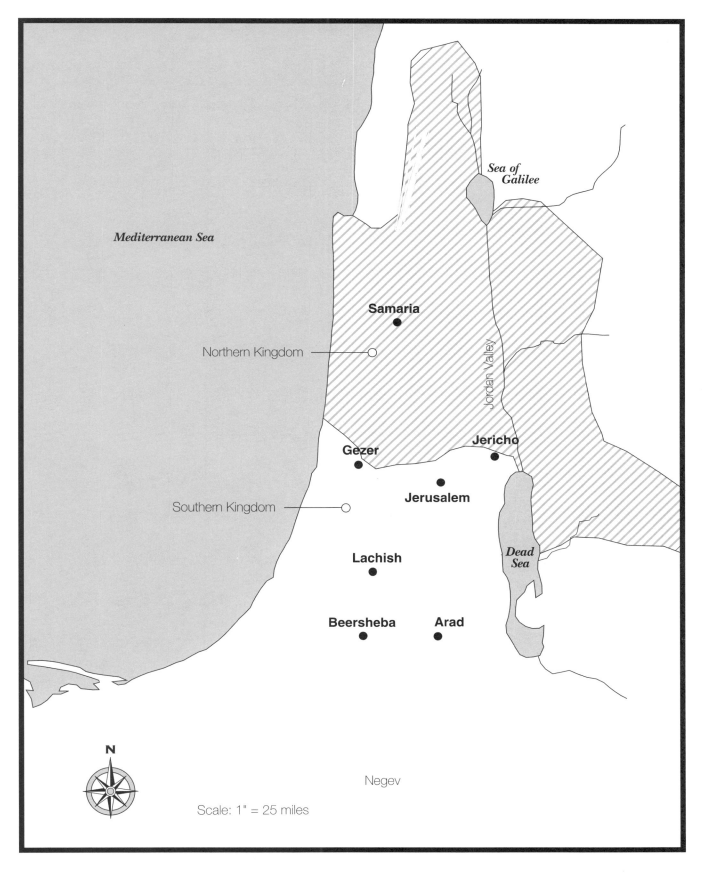

CHRONOLOGY
OF BIBLE TIMES

BC

1900 Abraham goes to Canaan
Isaac, Jacob, Joseph

1800 Joseph taken to Egypt, slavery

1700 Slavery

1600 Slavery

1500 Slavery

1400 Moses
Exodus

1300 Joshua
Conquest

1200 Philistines settle coastal plain
Judges, Deborah

1100 Judges, Samson

1000 Saul, David, Solomon

900 Kingdom divides
Jeroboam, Rehoboam, Omri, Ahab, Jezebel, Elijah,
Elisha, Jehoshaphat

800 Jeroboam II (Amos, Hosea, ca. 750), Joash

700 Hezekiah, Isaiah
Assyria destroys Samaria (north), Sennacherib attacks Judah (south)

600 Josiah, Jeremiah
Judah falls to Babylonians (586)

500 Nehemiah, Ezra
Jews return to Israel

400

300 Alexander the Great conquers Israel, Ptolemy rule

200 Septuagint, Dead Sea Scrolls
Seleucid rule begins, Maccabean revolt (167)

100 Hasmonaean rule, Romans capture Jerusalem (63)
Herod (37–4)
Jesus' birth (ca. 6)

AD

0 Archelaus (4 BC–AD 6), Philip (4 BC–AD 34), Herod Antipas (4 BC–AD 39),
Pilate (26–36)
Jesus' death and resurrection (ca. 29), Pentecost (ca. 29)
Paul's journeys (44–60), First Jewish Revolt (66–73)
Jerusalem and temple destroyed by Titus (ca. 72)

100 Second Jewish Revolt (132–135)

The Holy of Holies

The Holy Place

The People's Worship Court

25 cubits

0

L. RITMEYER

The Holy of Holies

The Holy Place

The People's Worship Court